ALL
THE
LOVE
YOU
CARRY

CHARIS ED

**THOUGHT
CATALOG**
Books

THOUGHTCATALOG.COM
NEW YORK · LOS ANGELES

**THOUGHT
CATALOG
Books**

Published by Thought Catalog Books, an imprint of the digital magazine Thought Catalog, which is owned and operated by The Thought & Expression Company LLC, an independent media organization based in Brooklyn, New York and Los Angeles, California.

This book was produced by Chris Lavergne and Noelle Beams. Art direction and design by KJ Parish. Special thanks to Isidoros Karamitopoulos for circulation management.

Visit us at thoughtcatalog.com and shopcatalog.com.

Made in the United States of America.

ISBN 978-1-949759-51-8

I

when love is found…

LOVE
& LIFE

The love you have been searching for, you already carry inside your heart. How long will you wait before you demand what you deserve? How long will you wait before you ask for what is best? How long will you wait before you truly live? What does it take for you to begin?

You will one day look back and be proud of the ways you have healed, you have learned, and you have grown. You will one day look back and be proud of the ways you carried on, the ways you stood up to walk again, and the ways you stayed strong. I hope, right now, you're proud of who you are, where you are, and every single thing that you do. I hope, slowly, you're evolving to finally live your life's purpose, your soul's nature, your heart's reason, and your inner truth.

When you feel tired, when you feel weak, when you feel like you can't breathe, when sometimes the only escape is to cry and to sleep, when everything feels too much, when everything is falling apart, when everything doesn't make sense, when you feel stuck, when you feel trapped, when you feel used, when you feel confused, when you feel lost, when you feel like there's nothing worse than the situation right now, when you feel like there are no better days ahead waiting for you, when you feel like there's no more hope—let love guide you home. Listen to what your heart tells you and let the love inside it guide you home. And inward is the path home. That's why on days you feel unsheltered, you must only believe the truth, that your own heart is your refuge. So for always, please choose to love yourself. This choice has always been the answer, this choice has always been enough, this choice has always been the path.

You are not your past.
You are not your mistakes.
You are not your background.
You're not who others say.
You're not what the world dictates.
You are not the people who are
incapable of loving you,
they may be fighting inner battles
which you do not know.

You are who you choose to be.
You are what you do.
You are the decisions you make.
You are the paths you take.
You are the virtues you keep.
You are the philosophies you create.
You are the love you give away.
You are your purpose.
You are not what happens to you
You are how you choose to respond.
You are who you build
yourself to become.

You decide who you are.

Something awakens you from a slumber,
something detaches you from a breathless life,
something comes alive inside your deadened being,
something thaws your cold and frozen heart,
something revives your numb and anesthetized soul,
something places your heart in the mercy of another
or something places it in the mercy of your own,
something is not understood,
something cannot be reasoned with,
something changes what has always been around,
something alters the future that has always been bound,
when love is found
something unfathomable introduces itself to you,
something incalculable cannot be measured,
something holds you safely
while keeping you on the edge,
something makes sense, something gives meaning,
but something also breeds irrationalities,
something gets lost in the darkness of the abyss,
but something beautiful unexplained is also found
when love is found,
when love is found.

It only takes one serendipitous moment to change the course of your entire life. It only takes one cosmic collision to meet that one person who deserves to hold your heart. It only takes one decision to devote all your energy to your life's destiny. It only takes one plot twist to rewrite the rest of your story. It only takes one second to alter whatever predestined fortune that exists. It only takes one moment, it only takes one chance, it only takes one leap to change everything you now understand, to change the life you now live, to change the future you now see. It only takes one.

You are the only one holding yourself back from all the wonders life can give. You are the only one who holds the power to move forward or to retreat. You are the one in control of your fear. You are the one who decides to either let go of or take the hand of an opportunity. You are the one who allows what goes and what remains. You are the one who chooses what solidifies or what evaporates. You have the power to destroy and the power to create. Your potentials are boundless and there are countless roads that you can take. You either overspeed, go slow, or you hit the breaks. You are the sculptor, the painter, the writer, the conductor of your fate. You can choose to be ordinary or you can choose to be great.

Allow yourself to dream. Discover the depths within your soul you still haven't explored. Embark on adventures to seek your inner treasures still yet to be unearthed. Give yourself a purpose, or find the nature it has always been yearning for. Reward your mind with all the intellectual stimulation it has been craving. Go where your heart desires, where your life wants you to be, where your path wants you to thrive. In the tiniest of steps and gentle forward motions, move towards the direction of the kind of life you'd want to be living every day.

Turn your imaginations into truth.

Work your aspirations into existence.

Don't die without having turned
your daydreams into a reality.

Don't die without having turned
your ambition into an actuality.

May you live a life where you'll reach an ending never wondering about the things that would've, should've, or could've been. In this life, may you always attempt something extraordinary. May you live and love like tomorrow isn't promised because it isn't. May you relentlessly chase after your dreams. May you always embrace and coexist with all of life's uncertainties. May you be happy. May you live. May you love. May you be free.

Life teaches us that the only regret at the end of it all is that one didn't love boldly enough. So love. For nothing else matters. Nothing else counts. Love like your heart is a lunar tidal force. Love like you are both the sky and the ocean. It is only in loving that we feel the fullness of life, and it is only in loving that we are truly alive.

The search for true love must first come
from within, it's where the journey
of true love must always begin.

You're always one decision away from flipping the switch, from pulling the lever, from hitting that target, from pressing that key.

You're always one awareness away from all the answers to your questions, the solutions to your problems, the remedies to your ailments, the elixir to your poisons.

You are always one consciousness away from taking a different road, another path, a better path, or from opening a better door.

You're always one commitment away from the life you've always imagined, dreamed of, hoped for, longed for.

You're always, always one decision and devotion away from living the life you know in your heart you deserve. You're one decision away from beginning to live that life today.

Only change is constant in this life. People and things come and they go. But when everyone else has gone home and you are on your own, what remains with you? What do you value? Why do you carry on? Why do you keep believing? Why do you hold on? What is your reason? What makes you stay? What keeps you here? What got you up today?

Don't grow old with regret because you never placed a bet on yourself or on that special someone or on that house or on that trip or on that move or on that change or on that choice. If a life decision is, you know in your heart of hearts, positively and significantly life-changing, then what are you waiting for? What's holding you back? What's scaring you? Why are you wasting your time? What do you need to take that step forward?

Ask yourself what kind of life you want to live, because it is the ultimate question that will encourage you to change your ways. It will give you the courage to attempt to make the wisest decisions, it will push you to work hard for your dreams. It will force you to envision and pursue the future your heart desires, it will show you your purpose, it will motivate you to choose only the people and things that serve you, it will give you clarity as to who and what is best for your life. It is an oracle of the things that are supposed to be, it may also be the gateway to living out your destiny, but most of all, this question will bridge the gap between who you are now and who you are meant to be.

If you are afraid to take the leap, you will never know the worth of something and you could be missing out on all the beauty this life means for you to receive. If you think something is meaningful and it will make you happy, have the courage to take the jump. If the pursuit doesn't work out, take comfort in the fact that you did what you could, that you gave all your heart, and you didn't let fear hold you back. This way, you will grow old without regrets, you will not look back on your life with resentment, you will only be looking forward with joy and contentment knowing that at one point in this lifetime, you had tried to chase after something extraordinary. The attempt alone should be enough to make your heart happy, but the attainment only affirms the path as, undeniably, your life's destiny.

The greatest souls often carry too much love within them, and there is no other purpose for it than to be shared, to be passed on beyond the mortal body, and to be given out into the world. A heart cannot possess too great of a love for it not to overspill; that love will eventually be emitted, for love must be used, love is meant to be radiated and consumed, love must be diffused. So radiate your love away, for always, even on days you need it yourself. All the love you give out will come back to you and you will receive all the love that you deserve.

Love is you and I,
Love is where we came from,
Love is where we're at,
Love is where we're headed.
Love never injures nor wounds;
instead, Love heals, restores, and mends.
Love is where everything began
and Love is where everything will end.
Love created us,
Love is a place and a reality we make,
Love designed our beings,
Love is greater than any grief,
than any heartache, than any mistake.
In this earthly soil we exist in,
Love is heaven incarnate,
Love is you and I,
Love is beauty and truth,
Love is our redemption, our salvation,
for Love is the only immaculate force
that awakens our souls and keeps it awake.
Love is our rescue, our refuge.
Love is our purpose.

Let love be your driving force,

Let love be your energy,

Let love be your spirit and vitality,

Let love be your reason.

May you always base your life decisions, no matter how big or small, on the questions: will this lead me to the life I want to be living 10, 15, 20 years from now? Will I regret this later on? Will this bring me profound happiness? Will this bring my life meaning? What is my purpose? Is this a worthwhile pursuit? Will I be wasting my time and energy? What are my true intentions? Do I want this now because I feel fearful, insecure, and lonely? Or do I genuinely, sincerely desire this for my life with all my heart? Will my future self be proud of me for this and thank me later on? What is my goal? What is the end I have in mind? What is the result I want to come out of this endeavor? What is the story I want to write? What do I need? What do I really want? What do I value? What is it that really matters in my life?

You are strong,
for you are stone.

You are soft,
for you are flesh.

You are more than enough,
for you are you.

You are everything,
for you are truth.

You are Love,
and Love is you.

True love makes us
better people.

One of the most indistinct concepts in our reality is the culture of love. We all believe love is an emotion, a feeling, butterflies in our stomachs, or a romance everlasting but it isn't. Love isn't all the lies we've been fed in movies or in novels, love isn't dating or cycling in and out of relationships, because, at the end of it all, love is a skill. Love is what we do, love is what we show other people, love is what we practice every day, love is consistency, love is how we live our lives, love is the kindness we show others even at times they don't deserve it, love is the decision that you'll be there for someone regardless of what they do, love is unconditional, love is truth, love is the patience that you will support one with their growth, love is the acceptance of someone's past, present, and future. Love is the understanding of all the events that led to one person's character and behavior. Love isn't jumping off a bridge when someone asks you to, love isn't sex, love isn't flowers or candlelight dinners or chocolates, love isn't the exhilarating moments two humans share, love isn't all excitement, love isn't all feelings, love isn't all attraction, love is not just chemistry, love is deeper than all of these things for love is the choice to stay no matter the case, no matter the weather, love is the choice to remain because you've decided to stay with one person forever, love is mental resilience. Love is the admiration for someone's virtue not for someone's exterior, love is the admiration for someone's character not one's perfection because perfection doesn't exist. Love is the act of being there through the best and the worst, love is the promise that you will protect each other from everything that isn't good, it is a promise to protect each other from the cruelty of the world, love is kind, love is nurturing and never hurting, love is the silent presence of someone wishing you all the good things life can bring, love is the constant teaching and learning with another human being because it isn't love if there is no growth, it isn't love if one is being held back and only one is moving forward, it isn't love if one of the two whole loses themselves in another, for true love is a walking side by side, love is a growing together towards a common pursuit. Love is the permanent thing that is with you through the light and through the dark, through the ups and the downs, through all the weaknesses and through all of the strengths. Love is the one thing in your life that lasts, that's consistent, and that's good. Love is permanent and never temporary. Life is nothing without love. If there's one thing this journey will teach you is that life is synonymous with love. They are not the same words but they have the same meaning.

Live your days with every bit
of love that you can give.

Live your days with every bit
of love you have within.

.

And isn't it that the purpose of our lives is to simply experience being alive, maybe to rebel against all absurdities, or to further understand our humanity, but what's certain in this life is that we are here to love with all the love we carry, perhaps, even to give out a love that will linger beyond our mortal bodies, or give out a love that transcends beyond space and time. So love wholeheartedly, love with every piece of you, it is the only way to live our lives so fully, and to live our lives so true.

Feelings are the chemicals in our bodies, the neurotransmitters in our brains, and the hormones our endocrines release. Chemicals wane in time because as our body changes, so does our chemistry. Most of the time, we confuse 'chemistry' as 'love' and we are then mind-boggled as to how and why that 'love' fades in time. Most, if not all of the time, we confuse intense emotions as being the 'right path' and the 'right intention' but it is never quite so. The only feeling that you must listen to is the one that makes you feel enough. Please only listen to the feelings that make you feel safe, alive, worthy, and loved.

Your love and affection are a prize to be won, a rarity that must be earned. You must know that your heart is a privilege that must be pursued. Your heart is the reward that must be valued. Your love, time, and energy are the most priceless gifts you can ever offer someone so with this truth, you must understand that your love is not for everyone. Other people's incapacity to receive and reciprocate love is not your fault, some souls are simply unable to heal their wounds in this lifetime.

May you carefully filter who comes in and out of your life, who leaves and who remains, for choosing whom you give your love toward shows the world how much you value your own self. You must be wise in choosing whom you give your heart to, for your heart is gold, a wealth, a gem, and what you have inside you best. You see, all the treasures in this world and in this life are always contained within a chest.

Please choose the love that values you, grows you, strengthens you, and respects you. Please leave behind any kind of love that is the depleting kind, draining all the light inside of you. Please choose the love that triggers the overflow of all the goodness you have buried deep within your soul. Please choose the love that betters you, holds you, inspires you, keeps you, and a love that loves you too.

You love the way you know how. You love the ways you've been loved before. You love this much and you love like that. You love somehow, you love somewhat. But what does love truly mean? Love is a daily deliberation. It doesn't matter if it is yourself you love or if it is another. Love isn't how you feel. Love is the daily choosing, the daily committing, the daily devoting of this so-called 'love' either to yourself or to another human being. Love is the decision to simply love each day. Love is choosing to love no matter what others think or say. Love is choosing to love yourself daily. Love is choosing the same person to love each waking moment. Love is the choice to stay forever, to be consistent, to be loyal and true no matter the weather. In our lives, we are presented with many choices, endless options, countless alternatives, and plenty of possibilities but love is a daily deliberation that no matter what happens, you will always choose yourself, the same love, the same thing, and the same special person you've decided to devote all your love towards. Know that everything enters our thoughts, everything is processed by our brains, and when one has a resilient mind, one will choose love every day, every time, every attempt, every chance, and every change. Choose love always.

You have the capacity within you to create the life you've always imagined, you hold in your hands the ability to transform all your dreams into reality. Life can be cruel sometimes, but no matter how much life tries to take hope out of your grasp, you must remain resilient by painting a mental picture of the life you want to be living every day.

So imagine yourself sipping morning coffee, awaiting the sunrise, sitting on the front porch of the house you've always dreamed of settling in. Picture yourself in Musée d'Orsay admiring Van Gogh's self-portrait and more of the world's most magnificent works of art including yourself. Imagine a warm summer night sitting on the Atlantic Ocean shoreline under the blue Nantucket sky, the arms of the one you love wrapped around you as you both wait for the moonrise. Imagine a coffee crawl in Vienna or Stockholm, enjoying European city sights, holding hands with your favorite person as you both make fun of the absurdities of life.

Or simply imagine yourself, living the life of your dreams, living the life you have always imagined.

Remember in your heart that life's beauty is forever yours to keep, that the world may break you but your life is entirely yours to make, that there are brighter days ahead waiting for you, that there's always a way out of any pseudo hopelessness that might be blinding your visions of the future, that you are surrounded by love and you are love itself, and that the waves of fate is carrying you in its arms safely as you journey homeward.

After the sunset is the afterlight, and then the darkness falls, but I know you will continue shining in the twilight because your heart is so beautiful. Please never allow anyone or anything in this world and in this lifetime to alter the immensity of all the love you carry.

If Love is not the reason,

then what else are we living for?

What are we fighting for?

What are we here for?

There are many forms of love in our Universe but there are two main loves that stem from the human heart. There is a wrong kind of love and it is selfish, only self-indulging, conditional, possessive, and only exists to meet the ego's needs. Then there's the opposite of that kind of love, and it's a love that's real, selfless, unconditional, protective, a love that is nothing but kind, a love that's respectful, constant, loyal, trusting, and only radiates clarity and peace of mind.

You fall in love with depth. You fall in love with the soul. You fall in love with the character. You fall in love with their morals and philosophies that align with yours, it doesn't need to be a perfect alignment but there must be a common ground. You don't fall for the superficial, or the temporary, or the physical body, or the status. You don't fall for the chocolates and the flowers, for the candlelight dinners, for the jewelry and other extravagant gifts, for the sweet words, the promises, or their net worth value. You don't fall for their past, you fall in love with their present and their future, but you must have the heart to accept all three. You don't fall in love with their mistakes, you fall in love with all the goodness their heart is still able to create. You don't fall in love with their failures, you fall in love with their desire to rise again. You don't fall in love with chemistry because these chemicals will fade in time, you fall in love with your decision to love your person daily by keeping a resilient mind. You fall in love with them because they love you back. You fall in love because you are each other's everything and you were never each other's options, but have always been each other's priorities. You fall in love with their intentions, their desires, their hopes, and their dreams. You fall in love with who they are, not their 'maybes' or their 'what ifs.' But you must have full acceptance of their entirety if you are to truly, genuinely, sincerely love somebody. Fall in love using both your heart and your mind to prevent the two from a destructive collision. Fall in love by looking at the whole picture, not just the bits and pieces you currently see, look at all the angles before you wholeheartedly dive in. You fall in love because they give you happiness, not stress. You fall in love because you learn from them and they learn from you. You fall in love because there is growth to be found in the togetherness. You fall in love because the two of you together make you better humans than when you two are apart. You fall in love because together, you two make an awe-inspiring, glorious work of art.

The love between two people should be mutual, it should be reciprocal, it should be beneficial for both. The love between two individuals should be symbiotic, it should be the propellant to each others' growth.

Love is more a verb than it is a noun. Love is more an action than it is an emotion. Love is never a question. Love is always sure. Love is a conviction. Love is all the light you're capable of emitting hibernating deep inside of you. Love is constant. Love is truth. Love is you.

True love isn't 'falling' in love with another person. True love is a choice, it is a decision. True love is a daily deliberation. True love is understanding. True love is the constant choosing to be loyal to the one you have decided to devote all of your love to, and this devotion can be towards another person, a life purpose, or towards you.

Be wise to whom you give all your love to.

You can only give away the love you've already given to yourself. You cannot give away something you do not have. You cannot give away something you do not understand.

Prioritize self-acceptance, self-awareness, self-respect, self-care, self-knowledge, self-worth, self-actualization, self-love over anything in this world. Valuing your own well-being is the first step to practicing love's true meaning. To put yourself first is not selfish, it is necessary, it is freeing. To choose yourself is the first step in understanding how to love another soul. To know yourself is to glue together all your broken pieces back into a better whole.

You cannot recreate the kind of love that has been broken and then hope for it to be whole. You cannot model your expectations on a kind of love that never stood the test of time. You cannot find true love in someone who is similar to the person who has failed you before. The broken families we've witnessed, or the separation of our parents, or the betrayals of the people whom we've loved and trusted, or the wrong notions of love that we've been fed, or the failed relationships we've seen from our families and friends, or all the abandonment and all the traumas we all have ever been through and experienced are not us. They are not our future, not our definition, and certainly not our ending. They are but lessons that show us how to alter our course, they show us what love is and what it isn't, they teach us how to forgive and how to let go. The past can be a backstory but not necessarily the plot, the past is merely a lecture on how to prevent repeating history's errors by choosing a different path.

How you treat others is a mirror
of your self-worth.

How you love other people is a reflection
of how much you love yourself.

How you live your life is parallel
to all the values your heart holds.

All that you value is all the truth
contained within your soul.

Today's generation operates on a belief of 'I am incomplete without a relationship.' This is the wrong notion of love we must break and the wrong sense of self we must put to an end. This mindset breeds desperation and a functioning from a place of lack, not of wholeness. This is not the proper frame of mind to have when entering one of life's greatest works, which is to share your love with another person. Self-growth must be one's priority before one considers developing a relationship with someone else. How did our culture ever lead us to believe that another's love will complete us when we haven't even learned to harness the love we harbor within our own hearts and souls?

If you seek love with the hopes of it determining your value, then you are searching for love for the wrong reasons. Seek love because you've already recognized your worth and you only ever desire to share all the love inside of you that you've unearthed.

True love is growing together while being able to keep separate selves. It is a truth that you must first and always look to yourself for strength, this is why when another heart provides you with sustenance more than they provide you stress, you know the love is meaningful because there's purpose in the togetherness.

Why do we yearn for outside acceptance, external validations, or other people's affirmations when what matters, first and foremost, is for us to develop the deepest relationship of all and that is the one with our own selves.

Develop love with your own self first.

Complementary growth and mutual healing should be the cornerstone of two people bonded together. Love should be the core principle of permanent connections. As in everything, love should be the underlying philosophy as well as the solid rock foundation.

Let love be your reason.

Your body is not only your avatar to walk and experience your current journey here on Earth. Your body is a sacred mortal vessel meant to shelter your heart, mind, and soul. And to care for yourself is to protect the armor housing your spirit's home. And how do you care for your home? You keep it, you clean it, you maintain it, you do not disrespect it, you do not give access to it just to anybody, you guard it, you upgrade it, you expand its being, you carefully choose who can come inside, you wisely pick whom can take up space and who deserves your light, you beautify your home, you only better it, you do not hurt it, you do not risk it, you love and value it. Do not dehumanize yourself by giving your mortal body away to non-substantial relationships or to temporary connections, or to activities that threaten its integrity. What will your body and soul gain from trivialities? Nothing but harm. Do not dehumanize your soul by desecrating the vessel the Universe has given it in this lifetime by abusing it over harmful and meaningless pursuits. Respect your body, for it is made of elements that compose the massive planets and the brightest stars in our cosmic sky. Your physical body is celestial yet it is designed to die. Your mortal body is the vessel that will carry your consciousness safely towards your next life.

Self-respect is the solid ground on which your self-love stands upon and once you've mastered self-acceptance, you'll never again function from a place of lacking.

Never lose who you are in exchange for validations other people can provide temporarily. It is a waste of your time and energy to try to earn approval from others when in truth, you've always contained all the love and strength you need inside of you.

Never confuse
self-love with self-absorption,
self-awareness with egocentricity,
self-worth with narcissism,
self-esteem with vanity,
self-respect with pridefulness,
self-sufficiency with selfishness,
self-resilience with arrogance,
nor self-regard with self-interest.

The delicate balance between all these
lies in mastering the art
of empathy and humility.

Love yourself enough that
love becomes, at all times,
your only reference frame.
Love yourself enough that
you only ever inspire
others to do the same.

Something beautiful happens when your heart heals.

You find a different kind of salvation, another type of redemption, you find a new breed of strength.

When you heal, the love within you multiplies infinitely, more numerous than the stars in the sky.

When you heal, all the love you carry not only rebuilds but also solidifies.

The love in you will constantly transform you.

The way you accept your evolution determines how you love.

The way you love tells the world exactly who you are.

There will be mountains you won't move, oceans you won't cross, and skies you won't reach. The point is not to despair over the limits, the point is to become your purpose and to live your destiny.

Live for what you were meant to be.

It is a truth that to live and love is terrifying but these fears are nothing compared to the glory, the beauty, and the joy our hearts can have if only we are brave enough, strong enough, wise enough to live our lives wholly, for always, only in love.

Live in love. Don't fear it.

Depth in humans is so important. How can you look outward if you have not first looked within? How can you live in love if you do not have a profound understanding of it? And this wisdom can only come from your heart's abyssal depths.

Know yourself.
Journey within you.
Unearth all the love you have within.

True love sets itself apart,
true love is outside of the common,
true love resides beyond the convention,
the truest love defies known notions, held
customs, or long-held traditions.
True love isn't all emotions,
true love, in truth, is devotion,
the truest love is a creed, a commitment,
a doctrine, a decision, a conviction.

So what do you release your energy for?
Where do you emit your light?
To whom do you radiate your love towards?
Aside from the world, I hope
back to your heart,
may you also redirect your love
back towards your own heart.

True love is when you have mastered the art of loving yourself. It is only through this mastery that you'll be capable of loving someone else. You'll find the right love once you stand up for what you're worth. Only settle for all the goodness your heart and soul deserves.

When you've found true love,
that is when romance will follow.
Because true love is the commitment,
but romance is how you show gratitude.

Romance is the display of affection
because you're thankful for your person.
Romance is merely the appreciation
of having in your life, their presence.

True love is to commit to a person,
to choose to love them every day
no matter if the feelings are still there
or have gone away.

True love is to know the depths
of someone's soul.
True love is to read their minds forever
like a never-ending book.

True love is to write chapters together
towards purpose, towards growth.
True love is the loyalty to withstand
anything that could go wrong.

True love is to declare and to
demonstrate
that you'll never ever let love go.

It is a simple truth and an incontestable logic that if you are not true to yourself and aren't walking the path you were created for, you won't find the people who will accept you fully as you are, you won't find fulfillment in all the things that you pursue, and you aren't going to find the one person who will love you for being you.

If you stay in one place, remain unhealed, broken, and unchanged, you will only continue developing artificial connections, you will only be building superficial life moments, and only gain temporary happiness. Do not become like those who are uncertain of their life trajectories. Know where you are going, be certain of your truth and live it, hold onto it, and never betray your purpose.

If there is no path, you create one.
If there is no bridge, you build it.

The world won't stop revolving whether you are ready or not, the Universe doesn't pause itself for anybody. So, starting today, why not choose to divert all your energy towards pursuits that make you happy, nights that ignite your soul, days that make you feel alive, and people who love you back.

Life is too short to waste not living. Life is too short to keep waiting for the right conditions in order for your life to begin. There is never a perfect state to start being alive and feeling alive. The time isn't when it's better, the time isn't later, the time to live is right now.

Make sure you live your purpose in this lifetime, make sure you only spend time with people who make you feel enough. Make sure you pursue your dreams. And if you are to chase anyone or anything in this life, make sure it's your own happiness.

In this life, there are many roads to choose from, so many paths to take, this is why the most important decision is choosing which path to tread for there are countless roads that lie ahead but there exists no road that'll lead you back in time to retract an error, to change an injury, to revert a regret, or to experience what you've missed.

Make sure you choose wisely.

Find who you are meant to be.

Live out your destiny.

Experience all the beauty, the terror,
the laughter, and the tears.
Live like this is your only chance.
Live like this is your only time.
Live like the poems, the songs, the movies.
Live as if you've never been alive.

True love isn't losing yourself in another and asking another soul to sacrifice parts of themselves for you.

True love is the merging of two lives, two hearts, and two souls that then turn their union into a better, more beautiful, purposeful whole.

Anything of value comes at a price. This is why true love is costly. Because the cost of finding true love is the self-work you have undergone. Your relationships are the mirrors of the self-knowledge you've now come to understand. True love comes at a price because it can only be found when one has made the sacrifice to do the great work of meeting one's self.

If you constantly cycle in and out of temporary connections and non-substantial relationships, you must reassess your self-worth and question why you are stuck in this pattern. Ask yourself if you are trying to fill an inner void, or to band-aid loneliness, or to mask insecurities, or to gain benefits, or to simply pass and waste time. Assess yourself and be honest as to how much soul work you'd still need to undertake. For before you can deserve true love from a whole and healed person's heart, you must first heal yourself.

Your love is sacred and anything sacred
requires devotion and commitment.

Do everything with purpose. Enter everything with good intentions. Build bridges that lead you to better places, not lead you to retrogress. Form only relationships that are substantial and long-lasting. Because if not, what is the point? What is the point of wading your feet in high tides that'll soon recede back to the sea, why risk your life to swim in ocean waters whose waves are only temporary? What is the point in wasting your time and energy on people, things, and situations you know are not beneficial for you and won't be in your life forever? Remember, your heart is a treasure. Your heart is not a toy. Your love is precious. Your energy is pure. You must only aim to always keep your soul intact, and your heart whole.

You have a responsibility to yourself. It is your responsibility to choose the people, places, and things that serve your highest good. It is up to you to decide which ones deserve to take up space in your life. It is your responsibility to keep moving forward and choose those you must leave behind. It is your responsibility to choose which ones must stay and which ones must go. You have a responsibility to care for yourself by leaving connections that only drain your soul.

Be wise when giving yourself away, for to lose parts of yourself in anything or anyone unworthy is a price too high to pay.

Shrinking yourself or dimming your light will never help. Your main responsibility in this life is to be your truest self.

You have a responsibility and it's the awareness of your own strength, awareness that you can stand on your own by courageously walking away from situations that require you to do so. Responsibility to yourself means that you never compromise your self-worth, that you always maintain your self-respect intact no matter what's at stake. You are answerable to yourself. Only you can determine your worth. Always choose to love yourself.

If you are to lose yourself in anything,
lose yourself in your dreams.
Lose yourself to your purpose.
Lose yourself to your art.
If you are to lose yourself in anyone,
please never to another soul,
lose yourself only to your own heart.

Before you take one step forward, before you make any decision, whether great or small, before you react or respond, please ponder whether or not the result of your actions will bring your life either peace or problems both in the near future and in the coming years. We can never foretell the future, but we can always do our best in determining it. So before you embark on a journey, please contemplate whether or not this road, when you've reached the end of it all, will bring you either joy or tears, contentment or regrets, love or hope, strength or wounds.

Be wise because every choice you make, each action you take, each and everything you do or say has respective consequences entailed. With each word left unsaid, each opportunity missed, each love you've allowed to fall apart, each dream delayed, each reason not pursued, each purpose forgotten, each person taken for granted, each goal left unfinished, each ambition left behind, each potential wasted is a life you've lost, a life you've left unlived, and a life you've left to ashes.

To have a kind and loving heart is to also possess the wisdom to discern between those who love you and those who can potentially hurt you. To have an open and understanding mind is synonymous with the awareness that some people are more inclined towards their dark side, only there to drain you of your light. May your heart always recognize the ones who are only there to use you between the ones who are genuinely there to beautify your life.

Idealization of a person or a situation is one of the main culprits of heartbreak and disappointment. Our highly unreliable emotions blind us from reality and make us conjure scenarios of future possibilities or of potential that may never even arrive at an actuality.

You must listen to the part of your mind that tells you what's real and what isn't. You must listen to the part of your heart that tells you, 'you mustn't imagine or idealize,' but you must see things for what they are and as they are now, not for whatever else they may or would or could be.

The things that are right for you and the things that are meant for you will not be shrouded with confusion, only with clarity.

So stop idealizing and start experiencing. Be alive. Seek what's real. Do the things you've always wanted. Chase your dreams. Create art. Go to the places you've always dreamed of traveling to. Share your love to the people who also love you. Focus on your healing. Aim your energy to your growth. Spend your time only with those who value your worth.

Sure, live in the moment, but be mindful of your to-morrow and heed the lessons from yesterday because the past only used to be the present and the present will eventually become the future.

The past, present, and future all overlap. The three may even be parallel and may be happening all at once.

See, you've lived, you're living, and you'll be living all three lives. You were, you still are, and you will be all these lives.

II

when love is lost...

GROWTH THROUGH PAIN

If you ever find yourself in a position where all you can do is cry, if you'll ever be in a place where everything around you is falling apart and there is nothing else you can do but to let it all fall down, if you ever find yourself standing on an unstable ground beneath, if you ever reach a point where you question what you are even doing here, if you ever find yourself in so much pain you never knew a human heart can possibly even bear to survive, if you'll ever be someplace where you'll stumble and the world's punches make it seem so difficult for you to stand up again and rise, know I have been to all these places and I can tell you with all certainty and all heart that the way out is to get through to the other side. And there is so much beauty, so much life, so much wonder, and so much love beyond what's visible to you right now. You just have to hold on, you just have to survive, you need only push yourself to be powerful enough to rise once more. There is so much love and life beyond any of the pain we choose to grow from and decide to leave behind.

One day you will understand how it works. You'll one day arrive at the place where you are wise enough to accept that some people aren't meant to stay permanently in your life no matter how much you want them to. You will understand that some people are merely lessons no matter how much you want them to be your home. You'll understand that some people are simply catalysts meant to give rise to the light inside of you so you can emerge from the darkness. You'll realize that some people only serve as reminders of all the virtues you've already learned before. You'll understand that some people are merely a caution, a warning, a foreseeing of the dangerous road that may lie ahead if you ever make the mistake of choosing the wrong path again. You'll realize that it's okay to let go because the beauty not only lies in the pain, but also in the love you've expended and earned and all of the lessons you've learned. What matters most is that you've grown from the hurt and know that from every ending, you will pick yourself up courageously and begin again.

What greater force is out there but love?

You're going through all this pain because it is the greatest catalyst, it is the fuel to your growth, and there is a lesson that must be learned. You're going through all the ache because sometimes, you linger far too long in complacency accepting the familiar and you need a little push, the hurt being that gentle nudge reminding you to move, to change, to become, to transition, to metamorphose, to walk forward onto better things, to settle only for the extraordinary, to never settle for less than you deserve, to leave the place where you're not nurtured, to leave the place where you're unwanted, to burn the bridges that turn out to be unneeded, to leave behind people who had your soul depleted, to astound yourself of your potentials, and perhaps, even exceed it. Believe you will find the people who will appreciate your worth, you will arrive at the place where your best will be brought forth, only if you have the courage to take the next steps forward after the push.

I hope you forgive yourself for all of the times you chose to remain in a love you didn't deserve.

If you ever need to apologize to anyone today, apologize to yourself. And after the apologies come forgiveness. So forgive yourself for allowing things you don't deserve to linger in your life far longer than they should've stayed. Forgive yourself on days you were too hard on yourself. Forgive yourself for all the self-doubt you've greeted to come and build a home inside your head. Forgive yourself for allowing some people to make you question your worth. Forgive yourself for letting some people make you ask the question if you're enough. Forgive yourself for allowing some people to make you wonder if there's anything wrong with you. Forgive yourself for giving some people far too many chances before you finally recognized that all they can offer are disappointments, failure, and hurt. Forgive yourself for being too kind, too loving, too trusting that it sometimes ends up causing you pain. Forgive yourself for previously believing you deserve half-measures. Forgive yourself for pouring all of your love into a cup that simply can never be filled because its breakages are too irreparable, its damages too great, leaving yours depleted and empty. Know you can always refill your cup again by redirecting all your love back towards you. Pour all your love back into your own cup as it's always meant to be filled. Give back to yourself all the love you've always been deserving of.

At the end of the day, I hope you let go of those who cannot hold all the beauty that you are. I hope you let go of those who cause your heart pain. I hope you let go of what isn't meant to stay and let go of those who aren't meant to journey with you until the end. I hope you don't allow losses or disappointments to make you feel like you can't mend, because you can. You can always rise up again. And from every ending, once more you will begin. So please let go of what isn't for you. You know exactly the things that are. You deserve beauty. You deserve love. You deserve effort. I hope you always choose your heart. You don't deserve to stay in places where your world keeps falling apart.

Are they the best for you? If the answer is no then let go. 'You only deserve the best.' Let that sentence be your closure. Let that be the goodbye. Let that be the parting words you've been waiting for. Let that be the curtain call. Let that be the end credits. Let that be the funeral rites to all the memories you will bury. Let that be the final act. Let that fade to black. You don't need the last conversation. You don't need their explanations, or goodbye, or apologies. All you need to move forward you already carry inside.

When has the Moon ever needed our permission to be beautiful? When has the Sun ever stopped from rising in the East? When has the Universe taken a break from its expansion? As everything goes on, you will also carry on because you are more capable than you think and more powerful than you know. From this ending, you will pick yourself up, heal, and start over. You will build your home within. You will embrace your constant evolving. You will create a life that's inspiring. You will not be afraid to love again. Never let fear hold you back from feeling alive again. Live again. Pick up the pieces for you must live and love again.

You are holding yourself back from all the good things you deserve when you continuously give your heart away to people who can't appreciate the ocean depths of love that it contains. You have it in you to reclaim your heart and put it back where it belongs. Return your heart to your hollow chest. All the love inside of you should be yours first and foremost.

People come in and out of our lives as catalysts, or lessons, or answers to some of our questions. Some of our connections aren't lifelong, some are simply propellers to our next great adventure. Some people teach us what we will and won't allow. Some people show us what we need versus what we want. Sometimes, some people teach us how to love. Sometimes, some people leave so we'll be pushed towards our growth. Sometimes, some people hurt us so we will learn how to forgive because to forgive is to heal, and to heal is to be strong.

You might not know the reason why something had to happen the way it did, you might not have the reason as to why some things worked out and some things didn't, it might not even feel right how some things have ended or how some things have turned out, but it will all make sense to you one day. All will be revealed to you in its proper time and place. Then you'll see how life purposefully redirected you to dodge a bullet so you may catch the beauty instead.

When you've finally awakened to your worth, you will never settle for anything less ever again, or for anything half or below or short or devoid of all the love that you deserve. You will understand that it is better to be strong on your own, alone, and complete by yourself rather than endure anything or anyone unworthy of all the love that you can give.

When you've awakened to your worth, you will no longer accept half-measures, nor allow for half-hearted efforts, you will never settle for half-lovers or tolerate half-friendships for you know in your heart of hearts that you deserve a whole.

You don't need to seek love from another heart. You don't need another soul to build within you a home. You don't need attention from others to be complete or to be strong. You can build your home, you can be whole, you can love yourself all on your own.

Never settle for half-loves and half-measures because you not only deserve the world, but the entire Universe. Your love is too pure and too precious to be wasted on people who do not understand its depths. Do not waste your time and energy on people who are incapable of matching the great love you contain inside your entire being. The right person will find you, the love of your life will arrive, and you'll effortlessly know it's meant to be because theirs is a love that will exceed all the love you carry.

If you're lonely on your own,
what makes you think another
person can make you happy?

If you don't feel enough or whole,
what makes you think what will
complete you is another soul?

Never look for your worth
in another human being, for
it's impossible to find it there.

Contained inside you is all the love
and resilience you will ever need.
No need to look anywhere else,
you only need to look within.

You never ever have to put up with anything that does not make you happy or put up with anyone who does not make you feel enough. You have the power to walk away from anyone or anything not serving your highest good. Your kind heart gives love away so effortlessly but this doesn't mean you have to accept what you don't deserve. To love genuinely means to understand another soul but it doesn't mean you'd have to endure someone unworthy. The right love will always treat you properly. True love will never do you wrong.

Love should never ever hurt. Stop believing the lie that to love is to be ready for loss. The ones we love and who truly love us back will never ever leave. The truth is, real love only ever makes you whole. True love, when it finds you, will never ever let you go.

You never ever have to convince anyone of your worth. You never ever have to prove yourself to earn someone else's approval. Your time shouldn't be spent trying to change others in exchange for their love. One of your goals in this life is to grow and evolve into the best version of who you are. Your focus shouldn't be to change your mold to fit into their shape. The right people will match you like a correct puzzle piece. The right people will appreciate you. The right people will stay. The right people don't need to be convinced nor changed. The right people wouldn't want to see you any other way. The right people will value you and accept you for all that you are and all that you aren't.

So find your people. If you're here, it follows they're also out there. Believe that the souls with a beautiful heart and mind like yours are alive, you need only to look more closely. Go out there and find your community. Find the others. Find the dreamers. Go out there and seek meaningful connections, deep conversations, and life-changing moments. Go out and search for your place of safety because your refuge is out there. It exists. Your sanctuary and your people, they all exist.

The temporary people in your life are your lessons. They aren't meant to stay forever inside your heart. They are simply the catalysts for your next flight upward, your next life stage, your next adventure. Maybe they were meant for you at that particular point in time for you to learn but they weren't meant to linger in your life for far longer than you had wanted them to stay.

It is painful when a relationship comes to an end but it ends for a reason and that reason is your growth. This growth is the path to strengthening your self-worth so you may meet your next self. Because to live is to constantly evolve, to develop, to transform, and if a soul chooses to remain unhealed, all they'll ever arrive at to experience is a void, hollow, aimless, purposeless, unfulfilled life.

So have gratitude for the people you have loved and lost however long or fleeting their stay in your life has been. This gratitude you entwine with the letting go will teach you to love and appreciate the people you have when you have them, it will teach you to never take anyone or anything for granted, it will teach you acceptance of everything beyond your control, it will teach you to grow in the stillness, it will teach you how to live with peace, it will teach you how to live with grace.

By letting go of people and things you cannot change and those you know don't serve your highest good, you automatically make room for better things, you pave the way for your superior life, you open finer doors, you go down greater roads, you make space in your heart for healthier connections, you stay healed, you stay whole, you stay in control.

Never ever allow yourself to be treated like a choice, like an option, like an alternative. With head high, walk away the moment you start to feel this way and never look back. There can never be any sound justification to stay in a connection such as this. You decide your worth. You decide the kind of relationships you stay for. You choose the relationships you nurture. You decide the relationships you endure.

Going in and out of non-substantial, artificial, temporary relationships is dehumanizing to a certain extent because you delay and refrain from the self-work that needs to be done in order for you to evolve and move forward onto your next life stage. Your refusal to be alone to engage in the soul work that is required for your transformation will keep you stagnant in your current phase. Your unwillingness to mature and change will keep you from experiencing all the love and beauty waiting for you on the other side of the mountain.

Cycling in and out of superficial connections is never the point of healing, it is never where growth can come from. Another person can never serve as a bandage to all the wounds and traumas you need to mend, nor can they be the solution to all the faulty familiarities, wrong patterns, and harmful cycles you'd need to break.

The answer is you. The answer can be found within you. The healing can only come from you. The decision to change is yours. You are the only source of your willingness to grow. The love you keep on searching for and asking for from others have always lived inside of you.

So let your own love heal you. Let it change you. Let it bring out all the goodness you have within. Let it transform you into becoming a light. Heal now. Heal here. Do not carry the wounds over to your next life.

One of the most painful roads out there
is the need for a certain love to be set free
because some souls were destined to collide
but are not destined to be.

Losing yourself in someone happens in the smallest of ways. It starts with you pretending to be someone else only to be compatible with them, which then leads you into attempting to mold your shape into someone you're not in order to fit their life, which eventually ends up with you sacrificing your time, energy, potential, and sometimes, even your own heart.

May you learn the art of walking away the moment you begin to recognize the sacrifices you aren't supposed to be making for someone else. True love will never ask you to abandon your true self, most especially not your worth. Real and meaningful relationships will only make you want to respect yourself.

If a person you care about walks out of your life, let them go, for they are doing you a service by revealing their true colors and intentions. Do not take it personally, for them walking away is a reflection of their inner struggles, weaknesses, issues, and insecurities, not of you. It is because of these reasons that you must forgive them all the more. After the forgiveness, never dwell on the thought again. You must only carry on and grow, continue increasing your value, keep learning, move forward, and live. They showed you what love isn't, let the right people show you what love truly means.

All losses are a kind of testing, a kind of healing, a kind of awakening to open your eyes to the immensity of how much love your heart can hold.

At the end of it all, you must know that no one else can help you in this life but you and you alone. This is an important truth you must understand and once you've awakened to it, you will see the beauty of having within you everything you ever need, you will find inside of you the strength to steer your fortune towards the destination you desire. Yes, there will be days you may feel heartbreakingly lonely and these are the days when you will be blinded by the impulse and longing to rely on something external other than your own heart. These are the kinds of days when you will feel the craving to attach yourself to another human being. Know that these moments are life's greatest tests, for these important events will either lead you to your breakthrough or towards a painful struggle. The reasonable thing to do during these times is to choose for yourself what's best. And of course, what else is better than the conscious decision to always love yourself.

It can always turn out to be
worse than what it already is.
So, endure the cold,
defy the odds,
ride the waves,
weather the hurricane,
brave the elements.
You'll get through,
you'll overcome
as you always do.
You can never drown
in the floods of despair,
for you are an ocean,
you are water,
you are the storm.

You may feel broken today
as if your heart is shattered
into thousands of pieces
but one day you will welcome
a sunrise where you will feel whole
and where you will realize that
you were never really broken
in the first place, you were simply
learning how to become strong.

Let go of the people who don't need to be in your life, people who don't deserve a space within your precious, loving heart. Leave behind the loads weighing you down, delaying your progress. When you remove the unnecessary, the unhealthy, the unneeded, the right people and the right opportunities will begin to reveal themselves to you. Believe you can let go. Believe in what your strength can do. Believe in your own growth. Believe in your own truth.

You are subconsciously choosing what you have the capacity of changing and yet you do not alter it. You keep choosing what you allow to happen, what you permit to continue, what you enable to unfold. Once you decide to cut off the unnecessary and to let go of the inessential, only then do you consciously choose what's best for your life and for yourself.

Once you start doubting your worth and you begin to question what you deserve, when your relationship with another starts to stir feelings of uncertainty because you find yourself crippled emotionally, it is then as clear as day that it's time for you to walk away. Save yourself the remaining pain. Remember that true love nurtures, true love doesn't drain.

Never ever waste a thought, or time, or any amount of energy towards people who are unable to reciprocate the same intensity of the love that you give. You must know that some people are simply incapable of love, loyalty, or commitment and it is not your fault, it is their own burden to bear. You can never love someone into their healing if they are unwilling to rebuild themselves. You cannot love someone into their own growth if they are unwilling to meet their evolution. You did not give up on them, you are merely practicing self-preservation. And to choose yourself is brave, it is something you must be proud of and you mustn't feel ashamed. After all, to prioritize yourself over another is the best way to look after your soul. You are not being selfish when you choose yourself, you are merely choosing to stay whole.

Even though most days you're sure of yourself, there will be days self-doubt will creep in. You'll go through days when you, yourself, will question all the virtues you have built within. On days such as these, let the stillness be your refuge. In the stillness, ask yourself what you value most in your life. Once you've found your values once more, you will be returned to your center. You will regain your balance. You will be in control of your gravity again. You will know where to go. You will be one with strength. You will be one with your truth. You will start over. You will be better. You will be at your best.

The hurt, the doubts, and the questions are there to open your eyes to see that the loneliest place on this Earth is to share a bed with somebody who doesn't make you feel enough, or to share the most intimate parts of yourself with someone who doesn't make your soul feel alive, or to build a life with someone who doesn't make you feel as loved. It is far, far better to be on your own, alone, investing in the greatest work of all, which is to love yourself, than to be in a 'so-called' relationship with somebody and yet still feel solitary and unhappy.

Loneliness isn't living by yourself or eating out alone. Loneliness is waking up at 3 AM to find someone asleep beside you who, despite their presence, makes you feel unloved. Loneliness is the yearning that you deserve far better than what you're struggling to endure.

Sometimes, your love will not be returned to you for whatever earthly reason, but that doesn't mean it is any less valuable, it only means something or someone far, far greater deserves that love from you. You must never forget that you can always redirect all the love inside your heart back towards you.

Love isn't staying in a relationship, enduring and tol-
erating a treatment you know you do not deserve only
to prove your affection to the other person. Love is
respecting yourself enough to take accountability for
your own welfare. Love is having the understanding
that by honoring your worth, you show the world
your true value, you teach others how to treat you
and you enlighten others how to love themselves too.

It's okay that it ended, you did everything you could do. It's okay that it didn't work, you gave it everything you ever have. It's okay to let go, you tried. It's okay to say goodbye, there will be new hellos. It's okay to forget but keep with you the lessons. It's okay that it's over, there will be better things ahead. It's okay my dearest, it's okay, it's all for the best. You might not see it nor understand it today, but in time, you will and you'll be thankful it all happened that way. The answers will be shown to you in due time if you don't know them yet today. Meanwhile, let the tears fall, let the pain run its course, let the loss change you, let it uncover and unravel all the strength you have inside of you. It's not that you should've attempted harder, it's not that you should've given more effort, it's not that you should've put up with it for just a tad bit longer, it's not that you should've tolerated it for maybe just a little bit more. It's not a loss if it opened up your eyes, if it awakened your mind, if it reconstructed everything you've ever believed in, if it revised all your long-held doctrines, if it remodeled your view of love and hope, if it reorganized all your detached puzzle pieces and reshaped them into a whole new artwork. It isn't a loss, my dearest, if it contributed to transforming you into the best render of the solid rock foundation you have always worked hard for yourself to be. It isn't a loss if it helped you construct your inner concrete house and if it helped you solidify yourself as your own well-built ground. It isn't a loss, my dearest, it is a lesson.

You came to this world alone, no one's absence should make you feel incomplete. You will keep on breathing, you will continue living, you will carry on forward, you will grow and evolve from the pain.

Our souls go through an evolution of some sort whenever we overcome pain and suffering; our minds gain more wisdom, our hearts produce more love, our mortal bodies experience and process more emotions. When we learn, we grow and when we grow, we change. When our souls transform, we are not the same, we become an entirely different masterpiece. Any authentic growth means to turn into someone always open to positive change, to reshape into someone who, from pain, unlocks new capacities and new reference frames.

When you evolve into your highest self, everything in your life will change.

Pain is the gateway to knowing.

Pain opens portals to possibilities.

Pain is the greatest of all catalysts.

Pain is the growth towards meaning.

Pain evolves you towards betterment.

Pain wakes us to our destiny's calling.

Pain burns bridges that need burning.

Pain purifies your entire being.

Pain brings out your best through the becoming.

Pain forces out your truth through the transforming.

Do not question pain. When pain pays you a visit, welcome it with open arms, an open mind, and an open heart. When pain shows up at your doorstep, believe that pain is only wanting you to change, that it is wanting you to improve, to upgrade, and to evolve. Pain is not the enemy. Pain is a teacher and a friend. Pain is the signal that awakens you to what must begin and what must end.

Sometimes, you stay far too long in relationships that do not bring forth your growth, you stay far too long in jobs that do not bring forth your progress, you stay far too long in friendships that do not bring forth your thriving, you stay far too long in binds that tie you down, that hold you back, that restrain you.

Sometimes, you linger far too long in places not meant for you because of distractions, comfort, or fears. Have the courage and strength to walk away from places where your love is unappreciated, where your soul isn't nurtured, where your mind isn't stimulated, and where your entire being doesn't evolve.

Walk away from anything that doesn't bring forth your joy because in this life, it is your right to be happy. It is your right to live your life genuinely, deeply, and completely. It is your right to live not in halves, but in whole. You mustn't live your life in parts, but only in full.

Walk away from the nonsense.

Walk only towards what matters to you.

Allow pain to be the catalyst that changes you, allow it to push you to seek only what's real and what's lasting, let it urge you to search for your soul's truth and meaning, allow it to grow you into your highest being.

Allow pain to break you then heal you. Pain is the nudge and discomfort that will show you which things you are enduring that are undeserving of you. Pain is the force that will compel you to walk away from anything or anyone unworthy of your love, energy, and truth.

Pain is your awakening but it is up to you to always keep your eyes wide open.

Pain will burn the bridges that need burning, pain will cut the cords to all your unhealthy attachments, pain will make you see more clearly things you couldn't see before, pain will teach you lessons until you've turned them all into second nature.

Pain will bring out the truth in you, the love in you, the best in you. See, fire purifies gold and pressure creates diamonds. Pain will hurt you but it will also grow you.

There are days that feel so unkind, days when every piece of you is aching, days when the hurt feels so debilitating, days when every cell in your body is building intimacy with affliction. These are exactly the days you must endure for you will only come out of it stronger. So let pain course through your veins, let it burn through your skin, flow through your body like electricity, rush through you like adrenaline, flood through you like rain, and sweep through you like fire. Grow close to the pain and keep in mind that pain is your perpetual friend, for it only intends to open your eyes to show you everything you need to learn.

There is so much wisdom to be found in suffering. And if you let this fire burn you to completion, like a Phoenix, you'll emerge as a stronger whole capable of things you weren't capable of before. So grow. Renew. Progress. Be reborn. Rise.

Do you sometimes wish your pain away because it feels unbearable and you simply hope for it to end without you having to go through the fire? Know there is no shortcut towards the resolution, only the path. And that path is your growth. Once you've become a better, truer version of yourself, the pain reaches an end. The pain leaves you for the time being and will only revisit when you need to learn again.

No one you love is ever really dead even when they have left their physical form; they live inside your heart, they live in your memories, and they are alive within your soul. When a loved one of yours has left our physical realm, may you take comfort in the fact that they are no longer suffering, that they can no longer feel any pain, that no one or anything can hurt them anymore, that no affliction can ever befall them ever again. You may not hear their voice anymore, you may not be able to touch their skin again, you may not taste their laughter, nor see the beauty in their smiles anymore, and it's okay. Know they are around you, they embrace you and they are present in every element surrounding you, protecting you. A bright light went out when they left, but you can continue to glow as they did when they were still here. You can continue to carry their light, you can shine for them, and you must make them proud. Cry. Let it out. Express it all. Allow your grief to encompass your being, let it burn you like a fervent firestorm transforming you into someone else, purifying you into another self, a higher self. Let your grief be expressed, let your grief be known, let your grief complete its task. There is never the right sentence, no right words for the pain you are going through, and maybe something inside you died when someone you love has left our physical plane, but know that you can bear the unendurable, you can surpass the impossible, you simply must because it is the pain's ultimate task. For you to overcome and evolve from this dark period is grief's ultimate goal. Remember that this will not shatter you, one of its purposes is to make you whole.

Growth comes from pain.

Pain is a necessary discomfort
that forces us to change.

There is beauty in the falling, in the breaking, and in the ruins. The falling is also the restoration. Your tears are the rainfall that will wash away the blur and the unclear. Your breaking will lead your heart to the path that needs to be taken. The ruins will teach you how to build paradise out of the wreckage.

So let your falling claim your past self,
not your potential.
Let it claim all your self-hate,
but never your self-love.
Let it have your hatred, but not your capacity to love.
Let it claim your skewed views,
but never your standards.
Let it have the unneeded memories,
but never the lessons.
Let it take the darkness, but never the light.
Let it take all the lies, but not your truths.
Let the falling break you because the breakage will make you whole. And this time, you'll be a whole better and stronger than any version of all the lives you've lived before.

It is in the descent that you appreciate the flight path upwards,

it is in the dive where you feel the current going upstream,

it is in the plummet, in the plunge where you are propelled to fly, to ascend, and to rise as tall as the mountains and as far as the skies.

It is up to you to turn your falling, your breaking, your shattering into the catapult that will thrust you into the highest of heights.

There is beauty in the falling and its eventual healing. If you choose to see it, you will find beauty in everything.

What you believe to be your deficiencies, your weaknesses, or your limitations are but distractions from the goal. Never allow any of these illusions to blind your vision and determine your ambitions. Instead, treat all challenges as your source of strength, courage, love, and compassion. Turn your struggles into triumphs. Choose to win and overcome. Choose to be a champion.

You must be proud of yourself for seeing the 'real' in people. You must be proud that you do not allow people who hurt you to turn you into someone like them. Be proud you recognize that people who try to break you are doing so from a place of pain. Be proud how you always choose to be the better human. Be proud of yourself for always taking the higher road. Be proud of yourself for not quickly making judgments or drawing conclusions or painting assumptions about the people who are mean to you. Be proud that you know how difficult life can be and that people can react to situations differently, that some people choose to hurt others, but you, you choose to be kind everyday. Be proud of yourself for not harboring ill feelings towards the ones who did and are still doing you wrong, for quickly forgiving them but never forgetting the lessons. Be proud of how you're able to keep your head high in spite of the mistreatment of others. Be proud because you understand that the source of their mean-spiritedness is from all the pain they've been through and left unhealed. You must be proud that you are able to carry on being kind and loving, showing them how to be an emotionally mature human being. You must be proud of how big your heart can contain. You must be proud of all the love you carry, so please don't ever, ever change.

You have the capacity to turn your tragedies into a masterpiece. You have the capability to derive clarity from all the confusion. It is a paradox of life, but from the struggles, it is possible to gather new strength, to find answers, and to form resolutions.

Moving forward may just be one of the hardest excursions one has to travel, for moving forward entails growth, letting go, and looking in. But it is a path we all must tread, it is a wound we all must mend, for moving forward is journeying within and a necessary call for our evolution that we must begin.

So move on from your old self, move forward to meet your rebirth, embrace your becoming into the best version of you, allow yourself to grow into your own truth.

Moving forward may mean many things. Moving forward may mean moving on from the person whom you thought you'd be with for life, and it's okay to let go, not everyone is meant to stay forever in our lives, you cannot hold onto the wrong love, you cannot hold onto the wrong person, you simply must let go for the sake of your own heart that's been exhausted from giving away love that comes back undervalued. You must accept the inescapable truth that things and people change. You must only save your love for the one who will treasure it and hold it in the most proper of ways. It's okay to admit you thought they were the one. We all make mistakes, all you can do is learn from all the hurt and keep your eyes focused on the path that you are on.

Moving forward may also mean letting go of all the attachments, situations, and all of the things that aren't helping you achieve your highest good. You already know which ones are discharging your battery, the ones that are consuming you, the ones that are emptying you. It doesn't take rocket science to recognize what's depleting you.

So be brave enough to take that one step forward, for it will be the start of all good things, your best life moments will be set in motion by that one little step, this is exactly why, you must be unafraid of new beginnings, you must not fear the leap.

As much as you cannot change anyone,
no one else can do the changing for you.
You are the only one who gets to decide
when to grow, who you become,
and how you'll pull through.

Never seek solace from the ones who broke you for they are not the ones who can heal you. The source of the disease can never act as the cure. The ones who hurt you can never be the glue that can assemble you into a whole. Once afloat, do not swim back to what drowned you. If you need to revisit the ruins, only return to build paradise out of the wreckage and to find growth out of the brokenness. You have rescued yourself out of the firestorm, you must never go back to the shadows for you will only be burned again. You must only keep swimming upstream. You must only keep on rising.

Sometimes, it's all just a bad dream and you need only to wake yourself up. It's just a bad morning, it's just a bad day, only a bad week, maybe a bad month, a bad year perhaps, but not a miserable life. It's only a spilled coffee, it's not a flood of tears. It's only a missed train, you'll be late for work, so what? It's only January and you feel like you won't make it to June, believe me, you'll make it 'til December once again. It's only an occupational mishap, is your profession really what your soul craves to be doing daily for the rest of your life? It's only a rainy day, not a lifetime of gloomy skies. It's only a heap of laundry you feel exhausted to wash, it's not a pile of catastrophes or tragedies. It's only Wednesday but you already feel so tired, it's okay, Saturday and Sunday will also arrive. It's only a lost opportunity, there'll be plenty more, you still have hope, for you are still alive. It's just a sprained ankle, look, you didn't die, you will walk again, if you want to you can run or you can fly. It's okay to stay in bed for a tad bit longer, I know it's hard to get up sometimes. It's okay, you're okay, things will be okay. I know it's hard to believe it sometimes, but everything will be okay. Sometimes, it's all just a bad dream and you just have to wake up to tell yourself things will be okay again. Stay strong for the better days ahead. Hold on because tomorrow is a brand new day. Each morning is another chance to start again. Each time you wake up is another chance to change.

There's no need to rush growth, life isn't a race.

We all have different paths, you're allowed to heal freely at your own pace. But remember that in order to live a fulfilled life, you must willingly evolve into each of your life phases. And know that each transformation you consciously delay is a life you waste.

Don't waste your time on those who don't value your worth, those who don't appreciate your entirety, those who don't add beauty to your life but instead, subtract from it. Don't waste your time on someone who isn't ready for all the extraordinary love that you can give, or someone who is unclear as to what they want from their own life. Why not chase your dreams instead, why not live your purpose, why not work on improving yourself, why not read more books, why not go to museums, why not watch an old film, why not listen to some classical music, why not read poetry for comfort, why not travel alone and learn the culture, why not make new friends, open your mind to new perspectives, why not jump in that ocean, why not skydive from that cliff, why not climb that mountain, why not? Instead of wasting your time over the ones who confuse you as to where you stand. Don't waste your time over those who disorient you if you have a seat inside their heart. Choose to love yourself and be resolved in that.

Why waste your time, effort, and energy on relationships that you know will end up nowhere, relationships that stimulate you but don't sustain, why waste your time on relationships that are temporary and superficial, or relationships that are physical-based? Why waste your time on people who only give you the minimum when there are people out there who are willing to give you the max? Why waste your time on people who are 'almosts' when there are people out there who are 'utmosts.' Why waste your time on people who can't reciprocate your energy when there are people out there who are willing to share with you as much love as your heart contains?

You are not missing out on the people who can't love you. They are missing out on you. They are missing out on a love that's loyal, rare, pure, and true. Don't waste your life over those who are unable to hold a treasure who is you.

Maybe your true love isn't the person who makes you question your worth, or the person who makes you feel like you aren't enough, or the person who leaves you confused as to where you belong in their life. Maybe your true love is not the person you think you want to be with, maybe your true love is the one who looks back at you in the mirror with pleading eyes begging you to see your worth. Maybe your true love isn't the person whom you think makes you happy only for them to disappoint you time and time again, maybe your true love is the dream you've always had dormant deep within your soul, or the purpose you were created for, or the aspirations and hopes you have for the future.

Maybe your true love is the deafening echo in your heart reverberating the truth that you deserve all the good things in this world. Maybe your true love is the thunderous voice in your head screaming the fact that you deserve better than what you're fighting to endure. Maybe your true love is the music your entire being sings to you like a lullaby each night saying, "your worth can never be measured by anything with limits for you are made of the elements that compose the powerful celestial bodies in our heavens, so don't you dare settle for less than the love you deserve, never settle for less than the beauty and wonders life has always meant for you to receive, never be content with living only half a life for a life must be lived fully, not only in parts, never a quarter, never a half, never an almost, but a whole, an entirety."

Listen to that voice, that music, that lullaby inside of you that sings you are enough and that you deserve not just the world, but the entire Universe. Maybe yourself is your truest love for true love will only want all the best for you. True love will hold you. You will never be too much, you will be right, you will be enough. True love will never hurt you. True love will stay. Your true love is you.

Only settle for a love that makes you happy, a love that inspires you to be your best, a love that pushes you to chase your dreams, a love that continues to teach, a love that evolves you for the better, a love that stays and will never ever leave.

It's better to be alone than be with the wrong one.
It's better to be alone than endure a love you don't
deserve.

Let them go. Let them make their mistakes.
Let them take you for granted.
Sooner or later, they will realize what they lost.

People never change until it's too late
that's why regrets are never at the beginning,
regrets are always found at the end.

Respect yourself enough by walking away from
anything not worthy of your energy and love.

You will be the greatest regret in the end by anyone
who did not appreciate your heart.

Something powerful happens when you allow grief to run through you, to let sadness complete its course by allowing it to heal you day by day. It is powerful because in healing, you find resilience and the path to loving yourself.

Healing is the part of your story where you are living between what it used to be and what's supposed to be. Allow the healing to rebuild you into a different entirety. Then, you'll one day arrive at the place where you are a stronger being. So embrace your healing. For healing is the path. The healing is the journey. The journey is the destination.

You must never feel sorry for yourself if you are not appreciated for all that you are, instead, you must feel sorry for those who are unable to see all the love you have inside. You must feel sorry for those who will never experience how it is to be loved by a magnificent heart such as the one you house inside your chest. You must feel sorry for those whose world is small and will remain to be because they will never experience the Universe that is all that you are. Forgive them. Some people are simply unhealed, overwhelmed, afraid, and unprepared for all the love you have they can never match nor give back. It is not your primary duty to fill an empty cup nor to supply love where it lacks. Your first duty is to yourself, to pour love by filling your own cup.

When a relationship ends, all the focus may be geared towards moving on, letting go, and walking forward. But in order to survive the separation, to pull through, to get over the heartache, the ugliness of a break-up must also be confronted. You must come to terms with the fact that the relationship didn't work because there is an important lesson you needed to learn. You must accept the truth that you simply aren't the right one for them and they aren't the right one for you. You must understand that it ended because of some defects in the connection, and that in each other there exist flaws that both could not bear to embrace, that there are failings and deficiencies in the bond that was formed that both could not fulfill or meet. You must now process the lessons and adjust to your new life without them by your side. It will be hard, in the beginning, trying to release yourself from the attachment, but you can do it, this heartache is possible to survive. You must have the willingness to move forward and then everything else will be easier to decide. The smallest of things may trigger the most painful memories but a heartbreak is possible to overcome. So wash your bed and blankets of their scent, throw away their toiletries from your bathroom shelf, return all their clothing they've left, return everything for you must spare yourself of all the ache. But please never return your heart to whoever caused you pain because the antidote is never derived from the poison. So delete all their pictures from your phone, take down and burn all printed photographs, erase all the text messages and the voicemails, yes, this is the ugliness of a break-up. If you are strong enough to stay friends with them as you move forward, then, by all means, be friends. But never rekindle the fire they made you feel that used to breathe like summer but now breathes like hell, never reawaken the feelings that used to feel like sunshine but now feel like ice-cold rain. If it ended, then it means there was a mistake, there was an error in the bond, and if you try attaching, it will only ever break again. This is not what you want to hear, but this is what you need, this is the ugliness of when two people who used to love each other split, but now, at least, you have learned the lessons. Now you can be careful and wise in choosing whom to love truly. Protect your heart. Be strong. As you heal, be gentle with yourself. Most of all, as you move forward, never forget all that you've learned. Remember what you deserve and everything that you're worth.

Most relationships these days shatter and end due to the lack of real understanding regarding the true meaning of 'Love.' When one does not understand love's true essence, one has not grasped its foundation and truth. And the world presents us with countless definitions of it, whether it be wrong or right or just for the world's own benefit. Love's true certain meaning begins and ends with loving one's self firstly before one can be capable of loving another soul.

Do not mistake love with lust. Do not confuse love with fantasies and eroticization. Do not romanticize another person. Never confuse love with psychological and emotional abuse. Never use love as a justification to stay in bonds that destroy you. Respect yourself enough to recognize the differences between all these. Be strong enough to walk away from places you know you aren't supposed to be in. Leave gardens where you aren't cultivated, move from spaces where your love is not appreciated, and take your heart back from people who don't deserve all the love that you can give. You must find the place where your love rightfully belongs and keep it where it is well-received.

On days you feel so lonely and your heart feels like it is shattering into fragments more numerous than the stars in the sky, know that you can cry. You can cry in the shower, you can cry in the rain, you can cry in your mother's embrace, you can cry on your best friend's shoulders, you can cry to yourself, you can shout at the sky and you can curse the heavens while you're at it, you can cry to the Moon and to all the night sky constellations, but never ever make the mistake of running into the arms of a body without a soul all for a temporary sanctuary, all for a one-night comfort, all for a short-term solace, or for a momentary relief. Know you are better than this, you are stronger than this, that your worth is more than this.

I know sometimes the sting of loneliness can feel as painful as a stab of a thousand arrows, but you must let go of your emotion's compulsion to seek short-lived connections.

Lie down in your bed tonight, alone, and weep before you sleep, flood your pillows with all your ache and all your tears. Tomorrow, if it still hurts when you wake up, know you can cry again and again until the hurting ends. And it will, all pain eventually comes to an end. Until then, you need only to stay strong until the shadows fade away.

Viktor Frankl said, "What is to give light must endure burning." Even when it's hard, you must only keep on shining. For after the darkness passes, you will only come out brighter. Radiate your love to the world by enduring the scorching. Those hearts who overcame the darkest of nights became the brightest of all lights.

You tolerating from anyone anything less than your worth is you denying yourself of what you deserve. Be courageous enough to set strong boundaries. Show them you are aware of your own strength and capacities. Stand up for yourself. Stand up for your philosophies.

If you question yourself whether you're in an unhealthy relationship or not, be honest with yourself and do not conjure up justifications, if the answer is yes, bravely dismantle yourself from that harmful bond before you completely tear yourself apart. Walk away, move forward, and then love yourself with all of your entirety after that.

Promise to love yourself to the point you, yourself, won't recognize the better person you've become.

It's not your fault they couldn't see the radiance of all that you are. It's not your fault they couldn't see that you're valuable, you're precious, and that you're enough. It's not your fault for loving people too deeply, that it comes naturally to you, that it's who you are. It's not your fault your heart can contain multitudes, that your heart can long endure, it's not your fault your heart forgives so easily, nor is it your fault that you're so trusting. You only choose to see the goodness in all things, the potential in human beings, you see possibilities instead of problems, you see a promise instead of a barrier, you see a staircase instead of stumbling blocks, you see hopes instead of hurdles. It's not your fault you are love that grew a head and limbs and became a person, it's not your fault they are too weak and too small and too unprepared to receive all the monumental love and loyalty you have been ready and still wholeheartedly are prepared to give. So know that you can always divert all the love you carry back to yourself anytime you choose to, that the love you contain within your own heart is everything you ever really need for you to pull through.

The world and the people in it,
sometimes, will try to break you
and when they do, trust yourself
enough to know they can't.

Sometimes, we all need some tragedy to make us understand what we truly want out of life. Sometimes, we all need to go through a dark phase to appreciate all the light we keep inside. Sometimes, we have to be hit hard by life's punches to really comprehend what matters to us and what does not.

Sometimes, we do not understand the reason why some things happen, but everything eventually leads us to believe—believe in ourselves, believe in our potentials, believe in our dreams, believe in our heart's capacity to get us through life's hardest parts.

If you look at things closely, a person or a thing that you thought broke your heart really never broke it, all it did was open your eyes to see how your heart is incapable of breaking, for you simply have too much love within, more than you know, believe, or imagine. And your heart simply refuses to shatter, it simply reassembles itself back together, no matter the tide and no matter the weather.

You see, physiologically, hearts are designed to pump blood throughout a mortal body and the more a human body demands oxygen and nutrients, the more the heart delivers. So it only follows that emotionally, in spite of all the hurt, the heart learns to only love much stronger. Whether from love or from pain, your heart only ever learns to love much stronger.

When someone breaks your heart, don't rebuild your identity out of the bitterness. Instead, rebuild out of self-love and then you'll see how life's wonders will find you effortlessly without you even asking.

When you let go of what isn't for you, what's meant for you inevitably comes.

The right love will find you if you let go of the wrong people and the wrong circumstances.

Let go of everything not growing you. Stop holding on to whatever causes you pain.

Letting go of what isn't for you means to claim your brightest future. Letting go of what you don't deserve means you choose to respect yourself.

There is no sense in trying to change other people. If you feel a need to change somebody, you must realize, you are withholding the growth of your own self because you are diverting all your light, all your energy towards them. Growth is necessary to claim all the beauty life has in store for you so grow by letting go of those who don't know how to handle a heart such as the one that you hold.

Choose people who appreciated you the first time around.

Choose the kind of love that brings forth your best and doesn't hold you back.

You will be the only one to suffer if you keep on trying to build a love with someone who does not value your worth. Why not build a love with yourself first? Love yourself into becoming your life's greatest artwork. Then you'll see, the right love will arrive, the one who, from the beginning, will appreciate all that you are. This lover could be another human, or it could be your own heart.

Why do you love to destroy yourself, to injure yourself, to tear yourself apart, to crush yourself time and time again? What is the delight you find in that, what is the achievement that you get, what is the benefit you collect? Why do you keep on loving people whom you know can't love you back, who cannot meet you where you're at? People whom you know possess the incapacities that'll only break your heart? Why do you love to cry and to weep, why do you keep committing this violence against yourself, why do you forgive them but have not forgiven yourself, why do you embrace your wounds instead of mending them, don't you see how much you're bleeding? My love, my love, it's time to stop. It's time to open your eyes, it's time to come back, it's time to come home, it's time to return your heart to your chest's hollow hole. It's time to regain your self-respect, it's time you claim what you deserve, it's time for you to rebuild yourself so you can be whole again. Stop giving unworthy people all the chances they don't want, they don't need, and don't deserve. If you have to adjust yourself, if you have to change parts of who you are to fit their form, if you need to reshape, to mold yourself into a different frame for you to be fitting and appropriate for them, then they are the wrong puzzle piece, they are not the suitable shoe, they are not the proper glove, it's clear they are not fashioned for your beauty and for your love. Second chances are a mistake, third chances are a pattern. So let go, my dearest, third chances and so forth will only leave you stranded, it will leave you abandoned, unloved, wounded, and askew. Don't do that to yourself, there are far better things out there for you and ahead of you.

You can never change anyone, you can only change yourself. If you feel a need to change someone for them to love you, let them go. All you can do is live your life in such a manner that will inspire them to change themselves on their own. If they come back to you, great. If not, take comfort in the fact that you are, perhaps, both their greatest loss and lesson.

How much more outside force are you willing to allow to have power over you? How much more of the outside world's acceptance are you willing to allow to influence you? How much more energy are you willing to spend in exchange for external validations? How much more love are you willing to take from yourself only to give it to someone else? How much more of your time and effort will you waste in order to feed a lie that you are complete and happy amidst enduring what you don't deserve? How long are you going to be blind? How long before you wake up? How much more are you willing to give up? How much more of who you are will you change for someone else? How much more of your soul needs to die before you realize you deserve a love as boundless and immeasurable as all the love you carry inside? How much more? How much longer?

All the hurt, all the pain, all the ache, all the wounds are merely reminders of how much love you carry, of how much love lives inside of you, and of your love's capabilities. So instead of you sulking or moping over all the tears and all the injuries, let the scars be your reminder that it's okay to love people so great, that it's okay to lose sometimes because you'll win more wars by loving that way again. But you know, my dearest, you never really lose when you have that kind of love within yourself. You must be sad for those who freed themselves of you, they've lost the greatest love instead.

There is no price tag to inner harmony. Inner peace is when you don't allow external storms to affect the home you've built within you. Know that you are always in conscious selection of the external visitors you allow to come inside your heart. You may not be in control of their effects on your emotions, but you are in control of your responses and reactions. You are to choose if they are to harm you or if they're a lesson.

You are not weak for being forgiving, you are actually strong for not forgetting all the lessons that require remembering. So do not be disheartened by any loss, only remember what you've learned, that in anything taken away from you, there will be something greater restored.

Remember that out there are people like you who carry colossal love inside their beings, people who can love unconditionally, people who are loyal and trusting, people who offer safety and emotional security, people who only love wholeheartedly, nothing more and nothing less. Let this kind of love be your standard. Let this kind of love be your inspiration. Let this right love be your parameter. Never accept anything less, or anything that doesn't match all the enormous love that you hold. Let the right love find you. Let the right love keep you and never let you go.

Never allow any pain to stop your heart from loving. The heart is a muscle for a reason, it's built to withstand all the hurting and only ever becomes stronger through all the suffering. Never give up on love, never give up on loving, never give up being love itself, for the whole world needs it from you. The whole world needs more rare souls such as you are. Stay strong, continue on because the whole world needs your heart.

If you ever need to stop or pause your growth for them to catch up, then that isn't love. True love is a mutual evolution through learning together and is a 'walking side by side.' In a healthy connection, no one should be ahead and no one should be behind. You must keep walking towards your progress even at the expense of leaving some people behind. To outgrow certain people is an inevitable part of becoming, of evolution, of leveling up.

They say that you lose a part of yourself when you lose people who have been a significant part of your life, but the truth is, you lose parts of yourself if you keep holding onto people that, for you, aren't right. You must never lose yourself in another person. You must keep your self-respect intact, and your self-worth whole. Take the lessons and allow the hurt to turn you into someone better than who you were before.

Learn loyalty. Learn to stay. Learn to choose love daily. Build your connections wisely and avoid cycling in and out of relationships because our histories affect the present as well as the future. We carry our unresolved traumas, emotional injuries, insecurities, and issues from previous bonds that then subconsciously dictate how we handle another person's heart. These unhealed wounds impact how we cultivate all of our connections. It is for this very reason that before you enter one of the hardest works in life, which is loving another person, be certain first that you are healed and whole.

The problem with an extensive relationship history is that an individual subconsciously clings to the hope that the present relationship will be the restoration that'll heal the wounds of the past, not understanding firstly that the past wounds are the very variables affecting how one perceives the current relationship.

These past relationship histories also affect the way a person shows up in a present connection because people subconsciously carry over the emotional injuries, insecurities, and issues of the past into their present. So, instead of going in and out of relationships with people, why not build a relationship with yourself first, then build friendships, and when the time comes you're certain of someone's role in your life, then pursue and build the long-term connection.

We exist to experience life to the fullest but that doesn't mean we have the right to break other people's hearts or to damage others psychologically, spiritually, or emotionally; know that when you do these things to others, you also do these to yourself. We create damages when we enter relationships while we aren't ready yet. We create emotional injuries to others and to ourselves by going in and out of temporary connections. We do not exist to scar each other, we exist to care for and love one another as we journey homeward. Be considerate. Be wise in building your bridges. Be wise in handling your connections. There is nothing fulfilling in having too many exes. It isn't true you need to experience everyone intimately and passionately to find the 'right one.' Love and loyalty are still the roads to everlasting happiness. To find the right love, grow yourself first into becoming the right one.

Until we collectively acknowledge the damaging effects today's culture of 'Love' has evolved itself into, we can never rectify all the emotional traumas and psychological injuries it has scarred the current generation and unless remedied, this wrong notion of 'Love' will continue to wreak havoc on the ones next in line.

Let us turn the tides by learning how to love correctly, and this can be achieved through first defining the true meaning of love, not the meaning we assign it to fit our beliefs and needs.

Simplified, 'Love' is you and I. Love is everywhere. Love is limitless. Love is divine. Love is the entire Universe. Love is sacred. Love is intimate. Love is gravity and time. Love betters you. Love never harms. Love heals you. Love grows you. Love is loyalty. Love is a decision. Love inspires you. Love is to have a resilient mind. Love is transcendental. Love is consistent. Love is considerate. Love is kind. What other meaning of love do you have in mind?

There is no need to give up the most intimate parts of you, whether physically or emotionally, in the process of getting to know someone. There are limitless, countless ways that are wholesome to get to know someone's character and soul. There are innumerable empathetic ways to be close to someone and develop a connection, it doesn't necessarily have to involve sex or intense emotions. Maybe dating can start from friendship to save hearts from emotional pain. Building connections doesn't have to hurt, it doesn't have to be a game, it doesn't have to negatively affect mental health, it doesn't have to destroy peace of mind, it doesn't have to be a struggle or stress, it doesn't have to be disrespectful. Do not give up your heart too easily, the love your heart holds must remain inside of you until the arrival of someone worthy. You must be patient. You must be strong. You must wait for the best. You must only settle for what's worthy. You must only invest your all in what your heart deserves.

You are love, so, for always, be love.

Never ever question the immensity of all the love you carry.

Love is based on loyalty and respect. If you do not know love, you do not know loyalty. Loyalty in everything is important because it shows the world what you value. If in a relationship, you feel the need to betray your person by leaving them for another, remember the principle that 'all of us are flawed.' You chose to love your person for a reason, so you must always remember that reason in order to gain the strength to choose to love your person every day. Know that the new person is only interesting to you at the moment because you have not yet seen their flaws which they surely possess and could turn out to be worse than anything else you've already witnessed.

You must also take a step back to reassess yourself because your seeking of another only means you are still incomplete, that there is a void inside you that you need to fill, that there is a hole inside your chest, that you must still meet yourself, that you still must grow, you must mature, you must change yourself for the best. You must learn what love means if you are still seeking happiness from others, for the truth is, those who have found true, genuine love in another person have first found love within themselves. If you haven't found love within you yet, then you must invest in the great work of knowing yourself first.

How do you forgive someone who intentionally broke your heart? Someone who knew how much love you're capable of giving them yet somehow, still purposefully caused you an injured heart? How do you forgive someone who knows how beautiful you are yet still managed to let you go? You understand. You understand that some people know your worth, they see your value, they just don't know how to hold on to an amazing human like you. Some people are just unable to hold you in their hands because you are like the Sun, they burn from your heat and they're intimidated by your warmth. People who are unable to hold you in their arms are not in the same expanse, the same mindset, the same stage in life as you are, they may not be ready to receive and give a kind of love as constant as the North Star. Understand that you are a constellation and they simply cannot fathom how to keep a marvel in their part of the sky. They may seem like cowards and you must understand why, they simply don't know what to do with a majestic meteor shower just like you are. You must forgive them for not knowing how to handle a heart such as the one that you have. You must understand that you are the brightness illuminating the Moon, you are the typhoon, the hurricane, the storms, and the monsoons. You must know you deserve the whole world, even the entire Universe and they simply are unable to give all these to you, so you must forgive them for not being good enough to be with you. Thank them, even, for letting you go so the right love can find you. And in the process of forgiving, you must wholeheartedly let them go too, as you begin the journey of loving, embracing, and improving the one and only you.

You are meant to live for so much more, more than this, beyond the now, more than the tears, more than all the trivialities. There is something deeper out there, something more meaningful for us to seek. Let go of the past, let go of the pain, let go of the panic in exchange for peace. Believe that out there is a more purposeful life you are meant to live.

Take back your heart from those who aren't ready to receive your monumental love. Remember, there's someone out there for you with a heart such as the one you have. The right one will be ready, not only to receive, but to also give you the very same energy you give out wholeheartedly.

The day you realize your worth is the moment you let go of everything undeserving, this is the moment you start to walk away from the place of the 'used-to-be' and start your journey towards the place of the 'meant-to-be.' And this place is where you build something beautiful and something new.

A new heart. A new life. New art. A new love. A new you.

The only closure you need to move forward is the one that comes from you. Why are you waiting on another person's explanation, apology, or parting words when the freedom, the liberation, the path upward, and the decision to grow forward into your best self has always belonged to you. You are strong enough to overcome all the hurt you have been through. You are powerful enough to begin again and to choose to start a path anew. You need only to choose to. So choose to.

III

when love is you...

SELF-LOVE AND RESILIENCE

I hope you find the love
that you deserve.

I hope you find that love
within you first.

I hope you always radiate love, even on days you feel like you don't have enough of it to give away. I hope you always embody kindness, even on days you need kindness yourself. I hope you always have the strength in you to laugh at all the odds, even on days the tears are too much because you are falling apart. I hope you are strong enough to paint mental pictures of the better days ahead. I hope you are fierce enough to fight off all the tyrants determined to knock down your self-worth. I hope you are gentle enough to keep loving amidst all the hurt. I hope you always see beauty in spite of all the brokenness in our world. I hope you always forgive no matter how difficult it seems to be. I hope you never tire of loving, of giving away the love contained within your heart, after all, it will never ever run out. I hope you never exhaust yourself from caring about everyone in your life. I hope your virtues are so well-founded that you will only keep swimming upstream and may you be buoyant enough to always keep yourself from drowning. But most of all, I hope, that you love yourself so fiercely, so intensely, so aggressively that you will never ever need love from somebody else, that you, yourself would be the source of all the love you'll ever need, that you are the one who everyone runs to when they need love on days they hurt and bleed. Because you are that strong, you are that wonderful, you are that powerful. You are the embodiment of love and everything else that it means. I hope you love yourself so wildly that you not only heal yourself but also others. Yes, you are still learning, still growing, and constantly evolving, but by loving yourself profoundly, you're already complete, you're already whole, you are everything you need.

The kind of connections you build with other people is a direct reflection of the relationship you have with yourself. If you respect yourself, you will respect other people. If you are loyal to yourself, you will be loyal to your loved ones. If you are true to yourself, you will be true towards others. And if you love yourself, you will only ever love others with all the love contained within your heart. You'll only be capable of loving another once you've embraced all that you are.

When you value yourself, you value your time. When you value your time, you only give worthy people access to you. Use your time wisely and only give it to whom and what matters to you.

When you value yourself, you value your love and energy. When you value your love and energy, you only aim them toward people and things that are as valuable as you.

Prioritize yourself above anything and anyone else in this decaying paradise, you must put first what is good for your well-being and what is best for your heart, soul, and mind. You must first listen to the whispers of your own heart before you listen to the heart of another, you must rely on yourself for resilience because, at the end of it all, you will be the only one who will be there for yourself when everyone and everything else cannot be depended on. You will be the only one who remains to be there for yourself when everyone else has left to be there for their own. Remember, you are your own home. This is the truth no one can ever take away from you.

You are not here only to be comfortable and to indulge, you are here to live your fullest potential, to fulfill your destiny's calling, your assigned purpose, or whatever it is you want to call the nature and truth that encompasses your entire being intended to be brought forth, intended to be lived, intended to be shared to the world.

When you begin to follow your purpose, joy will begin to follow you too.

Do not listen to the world when it tells you you're weak for not meeting its perfect ideals, when it forces you to play by its unreasonable rules, when it asks you to settle for those that do not move your soul or asks you to endure those that your heart has no passion for. Do not listen to the world when it asks you to do these things. And in cases you are forced to change who you are in exchange for the world's acceptance, belongingness, or validation, remember, it is in these times that you must rebel the most. It is in these times you must be headstrong, stubborn, and resolute. It is in these times that you should love all the more all that you are and all that you aren't. It is in these times that you must show the world the beauty of who you are. You must show the world all the love you hold inside your heart and all the love you're capable of giving. You must show the world your power, your talents, your skills, your gifts. Show the world that you are rare and unique. Show the world you are resilient and that you are relentless in your pursuits. Show the world you know exactly what you stand for, that you are an unwavering rock. Show the world you are unstoppable, you are capable, flexible and you are strong. Show the world you are bulletproof, unshakeable, and you're invincible to whatever life throws your way. Show the world how focused and committed you are to your purpose and goals. Show the world how you are 'love' in human form and that you are beauty embodied. Show the world that you may get scared from time to time but you are always aware of your power and strength. You do not need to change, my dearest, the world can change itself.

The problem isn't if we can or can't, the issue doesn't lie in our capabilities or incapacities, the difficulty isn't the question, "are we good enough?" All human failures stem from our inability to recognize our own worth, our own strength, our own beauty, our own power, our own truths. So know them, see them, believe in them, know your value and watch your life begin to beautifully turn.

CHARIS ED

How beautiful is it that we are an unfinished sym-phony, an incomplete storybook, that the rest of our chapters are yet to be written down on the paperwhite blank pages of our wonderful, remarkable life. How beautiful is it that we're all imperfect, that we are al-lowed to make mistakes, that it's perfectly acceptable to fall because we can surely rise again.

How beautiful is it that we're mortals doomed to be undone on a certain future date, that we're going to turn into another energy form and do marvelous things once again in that shape, that we're all going to meet oblivion but before all that, we will first create.

How beautiful is the beating of our hearts in sync with the ticking of a clock, how beautiful is it that our souls never die, that our minds only ever continue to broaden, that our selves are ever-improving, that our questions are continually answer-seeking, that our hopes and dreams consistently are evolving.

How beautiful is it to simply be alive on this Earth, right this very moment, with all the mortality and frailty and fault and defects that exist within and without our perishable, earthly flesh and bones. How beautiful is it to simply be a human containing within us the strength to hold our own.

Who are you without the contents you try to fill your blank pages? Who are you without the money, the rush, the job title, the lover, the admirers, the friends? Who are you when it's just you alone with yourself? Who are you when your heart and soul, to you, is all that's left? Who are you stripped off of the world and everything else?

Remove your mortal body, what kind of soul is there?

Remember,

It is only in being alone does one properly heal.

There is power in solitude.

Aloneness is an art.

To master your heart fully is to be truly free.

Other people cannot fill your cup, only you can do that.

Don't chase after someone else's love.

Chase after your own heart.

You are your own life's masterpiece,
you are your life's greatest work of art.

There is no need to prove yourself to anyone, there is no need to convince anyone of your worth.

You have the power in you to survive, to adapt, and to evolve from whatever condition or threat or shift that life may throw your way. You are powerful beyond measure, it does not take the whole world to see this, you need only to look in the mirror and see it for yourself.

There is no need to prove your greatness to anybody, the most rewarding and long-lasting validations can only come from within your own self. You don't owe anyone an explanation whenever you're undergoing the process of becoming, of growth, of change.

There is no need for you to get hurt from rejections because rejections are a lie. The truth is, beautiful beings like you are only being redirected towards a worthy, deserving life.

No one else can place a value on your worth but yourself. Your worth is dependent on the life choices that you make, not your mistakes.

Gold has always been gold even before it got mined, and it's still gold, even after it has been refined.

The things that hurt you now won't matter weeks, months, and years later. What matters and what will continue to matter are the lessons, the transformations that built you through your darkest hours. All the pain will soon be behind you, remember, the present becomes the past, you are too amazing to keep focusing on your fears, you do not deserve to wallow in your tears, so grieve all the losses and mourn your old self. You have no time for the things that have hurt you, leave them now, prioritize living your best life instead. Please remember, you must always only ever concentrate on loving and always believing in yourself.

This is what strong looks like. You cry yourself to sleep but you get up in the morning and you go on with your day. You cry in the shower but come out of the bathroom looking like gold. You hold your tears and keep a smile on your face as you brave to face the world. You keep on loving, you keep on caring even when you need these things yourself. You keep radiating like the sunshine that you are in spite of all the shadows trying to overcast your worth. You continue walking even when you feel like taking a break, you carry on, you carry yourself, and you carry yourself with grace. But you also cry before you sleep, you cry as you embrace yourself. You cry when no one is around, you cry when you can, you cry when no one knows. You break down in front of your mother. You break down in front of your best friend.

You hurt and then you heal. You ache but you continue forward. You break and then you mend. You grow and only keep on growing. You shatter but you rebuild. It's hard but you continue on loving. You keep on giving. You stay. You remain. You stand. This is what strong looks like. This is what strong means. This is what 'strong' needs to be.

I'm so proud of you just for sticking around. I know this world can be such a cruel place sometimes; that's why you're so courageous simply by waking up each day and braving what's ahead. Know that your best moments are still waiting for you down the line and there are so many people who are glad that you are here. The world can be messy but it is wonderful most of the time. It's wonderful because there are still so many places to be, movies to see, books to read, poetry to experience, songs to hear, sunrises to witness, moonrises and sunsets to fall in love under, there are still so many words to say, people to love, people to meet, lessons to learn, art to appreciate, foods to savor, adventures to create and wild nights to remember, there's still, for us, a creating of a life to never forget. The Sun and the Moon are simply too beautiful to miss, so hang around, be here, please stay, the world is so glad you exist.

The world will try to change you, the world will constantly pressure you, shame you, hurt you, discourage you. The world can be a mean and nasty place sometimes in spite of all the beauty that it holds, this is why you must always be prepared to tackle any trouble, you must remove your blindfold and see things as you should. Realize that tragedies are always lurking around the corner ready to jump out at you at any time. Be on the defense, the offense, always be on your guard. Always be prepared to meet the worst. And if the world is trying to break you, be better than the world. Show it you will bend but you will never break, that you know fire purifies, that you know you will only ever be transformed into someone better by all the ache. The love within you will never allow for your heart to break. You're whole and whatever's intact that has solidified is an unbreakable, indestructible force to be reckoned with.

Embrace your inner beauty more than your outer or-
namentations, for once you've built self-love within
you, you become an unstoppable element.

You are not an adornment of life's superficialities, you
were created to exist as a vessel of love and because of
this, you must embody and emit love for all time and
for always.

You are not the surface. You are deep.
Do not seek outwards. Search only inwards.
You are not empty. You are complete.
You are not hollow. You are whole.
You are enough. You are worthy. You are beautiful.

I know how we are all being bombarded by today's society with the theory that self-love and self-care are the main players to achieving our greatest, highest selves, that these two are the cure-all, the solutions, the path, the way, the formula to self-actualization. And they are, to certain extents, only, we must confront their definition correctly, we need only to define them in their most proper way, in the way they are supposed to be understood and precisely explained, defined in a way that the meaning of the words composing these two concepts become the most effective when applied to our lives and to ourselves.

Self-care and self-love aren't the trivialities we know of today, self-care and self-love isn't getting yourself a thousands-of-dollars aesthetic makeovers only to make yourself feel different or new, it isn't going out for an expensive plate of sushi or pastry to justify consoling yourself, it isn't spending a night in premiere hotel rooms soaking yourself in bath salts submerged in the most luxurious of bathtubs, it isn't the extravagant golden-dusted truffles you think will spike your serotonin, it isn't the fancy, sparkly bracelet you believe will make you look prettier, it isn't burning your credit card thinking shopping can cure your soul, it isn't killing and starving yourself trying to be a vegan or a lacto-ovo vegetarian or a pescatarian or whatever they call all kinds of vegetarian, it isn't joining a golf club, a yacht club, or whatever exclusive club there is, do you see the superficialities in all of these things that your soul does not even need? Yes, you can do these things to indulge yourself and are acceptable in their own appropriate measures.

But see, self-care and self-love, truthfully, is the daily decision that you will choose yourself over anyone or anything in this world, it is the daily commitment to love yourself, the daily embracing of all of your flaws, the daily acceptance of your rarity and of your uniqueness and even of your errors, self-love is the reading of an exquisitely good book and deriving from it life lessons, it is devouring poetry and allowing it to make you feel, it is in the listening to the saddest music and allowing it to express your grief, it is in the appreciation of art and the application of it, it is in the acquisition of wisdom, in training your mind to be resilient, in practicing compassion, it's in overcoming the impossible, it's in creating art and so much more, it's in giving rise to your truth, it's in sowing seeds of kindness, it's in both the breaking and the healing, it's in the restoration, it's in fostering your visions, it's in nurturing the realest of connections, it's in cutting off superficial relations, it's in your devotion, it's in your growth, it's in harnessing your intuition, it's in listening to your heart and its intentions, it's in re-assessing your mind's reflections, it's in analyzing your deeper self, it's in embracing your darkness and teaching it to harmonize with your light, it's in the unlearning and relearning, it's in the shattering and then the rebuilding, it's in the speaking up and in the called-for silence, it's in protecting your spirit, protecting your energy, protecting your vibrations and your wavelength.

Self-love and self-care is nurturing your own soul, it is finding out your nature and living it, it is fulfilling your purpose and reaching for all of your dreams, it lies not in trivialities. Self-love and self-care is depth, it is the journey inwardly, it is the journey within, it is the feeding of your heart and mind, it is the strengthening of your soul's health, it is realizing that your own self is your life's greatest work and wealth. Self-care and self-love means a soul's journey towards becoming love's vessel and embodiment.

My dearest, please remember, before you settle for something or for someone, that you are too beautiful—vessel, heart, mind, and soul to only deserve half a love, half a measure, or half a whole.

You are not the same person every day. You are expected to learn lessons daily and be better than who you were yesterday, not better than anybody else. You are not the same person ten years ago, what are the things that you have done? You will not be the same person ten years from now, so what will you be leaving behind?

Growth is never linear, perpendicular, nor is it a steady inclination. Growth is the swerves, the slopes, the skews, the steeps. Growth can mean stopovers or reroutes. Growth is the drive to be better each day. Growth is to be certain of what you most value. Growth is the evolution into your highest self. Growth is knowing your worth. Growth, most of all, is being accountable for everything you lay your hands on. Growth is your own responsibility. Growth is your rebirth.

When you feel discouraged, when your spirits are low, and when hopelessness has decided to befriend you for the time being, may you be reminded of all the love surrounding you. May you appreciate all the love that's there, may you see they are simply waiting for you—the libraries are waiting to be visited, the books waiting to be opened, the words waiting to be read, the poetries waiting to be devoured, songs waiting to be sung, dreams waiting to be achieved, friends waiting to be known, lovers waiting to be loved, places waiting to be seen, films waiting to be watched, Broadway musicals to be applauded, geniuses to look up to, wrongdoings and injustices to loathe, mountains to be climbed, oceans to be swam, skies to be flown, the Moon to admire, the Sun to praise, lessons to learn, ideas to create, adventures to take, mistakes to make, beginnings to begin, endings to end, wounds to mend, nights to remember, days to be lived, wonders to behold, beauty to comprehend, philosophies to keep, time to seize, miracles to witness, impossibilities to perceive, impossibilities to overcome, goals to attain, projects to finish, paintings to be adored, cultures to be recognized, prayers to be prayed, trees to plant, flowers to pick, gardens to cultivate, a self to love, a self to cherish, a self to worship. You, yourself is reason enough for you to keep on going. So keep going. Keep on dreaming. Keep on living. Keep on loving.

You were taught the pain of loss so you can learn to build yourself as your own home, your own rescue, your own sanctuary, your own redemption. You were shown what love isn't so you'll know what not to settle for and what to accept, so you'll know what not to endure and what kind of love you think you deserve. You were taught heartbreak so you'll realize you are worthy to have your heart treasured and held by the right people, the right time, and the right circumstances. Stay strong alone and wait for the right love to hold your heart.

Please let your heart love like it's all that matters in this world, because how you love is a reflection of what is inside your soul. When you are sure of yourself, you will be sure of your decisions, but when you're not, your heart and mind will ever be so fickle. The way you love is a mirror of the inner work you've invested in yourself. So what kind of heart and soul will you be showing to the world?

Maybe all you need is the courage to be vulnerable and honest to the ones you love and who love you, maybe all you need to do is to confess your entire being, to show them your soul and trust they will accept it. Maybe this is how the most beautiful things begin. Give the people who love you the chance and the choice to stay in your life, do not make the decision for them by keeping your soul only to yourself. Share your innermost fears with them, open up your heart, and speak your mind. Maybe this is how forever begins. Maybe this is how the greatest of adventures start. Maybe this is how to live again.

You don't need to be solid
to be strong.
You can be like water,
soft
and can take on different forms.
Be like water,
adaptable
invincible,
gentle
but can also be
a current,
a riptide,
a tsunami,
or a tidal force.

You are what you love, you are what you give your heart to. You are the books you read, you are the poetry you write, you are the songs you sing, the food you eat, the friends you keep, the movies you watch, the drinks you drink, you are what you dream, you are what you think, you are what you give in to, you are what you are able to control, you are what you give your mind and soul to, you are what you surrender to, you are what you let yourself fall into, you are the artwork you are working on, you are the visions that you see, you are your ambitions, you are your hopes, you are what you do and not what other people tell you to be, you are what you evolve into, you are what you decide to become, you are what you work hard for, you are where you succumb, you are the choices you make each day, you are what you prioritize, you are what you give your time to, you are what you spend your days and nights for, you are what you preoccupy your mind with, you are what you allow to linger in your life, you are what you believe, you are what you stand for, you are the principles and ethics that you keep, you are the virtues and the vices you have in your heart buried deep, you are your friends, you are your company, you are what you surround yourself with, you are the whole world, you are the entire Universe, you are the things that give you joy, you are your purpose, you are whom you love and you are whom you emit your light towards. You are the compilation of all the experiences you've ever been through, how you stumbled and how you've risen up again. You are the collection of all the wisdom you've gathered from your past lives. You are everything that's good in this lifetime. You are everything you'll ever need, you are the source of all the love you yearn to find. So drown yourself in your magic and in your existence. Trust the process towards building the life that you desire.

You have to learn to say no and be firm when you say so. Understand as early as now that some men will listen to you as if 'no' doesn't mean anything coming from a woman. Never believe the popularity when they tell you the word 'no' is negativity. No, it isn't. No, it isn't pessimistic. No, it isn't cynical. No, it isn't dismissive. Saying 'no' only means you have self-respect, it means you know your worth, that you have boundaries other people need to recognize, it means you don't live to please, it means you mean things when you say them. Saying 'no' means you have the courage to speak up, that every word that comes out of your mouth is clothed in honesty, that your voice is enveloped in sincerity, it means you can stand up for the things you believe in, that you are not scared to tell your story without permission. Knowing how to say 'no' is one of women's greatest rebellions. So say 'no' when your entire body is screaming at you to say it, say 'no' when your mind is telling you to say 'no,' and burn down whoever refuses to honor that, whomever fails to follow.

You can find love anywhere, for love is everywhere: love lives in your very bones, it is in the stars in the sky, it is in the sunlight, the moonlight and all of their beams, it's in the waves of the sea, in the wind blowing through your hair, it's in the singing of the mockingbirds, in each letter of every written poetry, it's in every stroke of every fine art, it's in all the advice given to you by your mother, it's in the thoughtfulness of your dear friends, it's in the hospitality of a stranger, it's in the smiles on the faces of innocent children, it's in being kind to each other. Love lies in the tranquility of a river, even in the chaos of a storm, love is in the comfort autumn brings, even in the harshest cold of winter, love is in the warmth that summer gives, even in the dampness of spring, it's in a flower blooming, a new leaf sprouting, a tree firmly rooting, love is your very existence, love lives inside of you. Never forget how love is you. Love is you.

In this life, please remember, you are the only wall you can fall back on, you are the only pillar you can lean on. You are your own solid rock. You are your own home. You are your own salvation. You are your own safety. You are your own shelter. You are your own hideaway.

Everything you need you already have. You are your own refuge from the storm. You and only you. You are more than enough to create a world that ignites your very bones. You are strong enough and brave enough to live for days that set fire to your soul. Never forget how you are so wonderful, how you are loved, and how you are beautiful.

Master self-sufficiency and
wear it like armor, treat it as
an extension of your pulse.

You are all you have from the very beginning of your story until the day comes when the stars fall down from the sky. You are your own light in your darkest hours, no one else will be able to provide you all the consolation that you need but you, no one else will hear your lamentations towards the heavens but you, no one will answer to your cries but you, no one else will catch your tears when they fall but you.

You cannot rely on other people for strength because other people continually disappoint and make mistakes, you cannot rely on other people for guidance because everyone else is also searching for help, you cannot rely on other people's promises because promises have the tendency to break, you cannot rely on other people because most people are attachments and attachments are the very root of all our pain and heartache.

You can only depend on yourself.
You can only count on you.
You are all you have.
You are all you need.
You and only you.

Recognize which connections to cut, which ones are good for you, and which ones are bad, for in order to claim all the best life has in store for you, you must end all your aimless loops and relations. Staying in unhealthy connections will only cycle you back to all of life's pain and sufferings, instead of propelling you towards your life's greatest achievements.

I hope you still believe in forever. I hope you still believe things that are real, things that are true, things that are persisting, enduring, withstanding, and everlasting are still waiting out there for you. The tricky part is to find these things, perhaps the hardest part is the searching. But love will always be the most genuine thing you will ever find in this cruel, broken world. So you must never lose hope. You must always believe that love is real and that the right love will eventually find you and keep you because it will. Love always ends up finding the kindest, softest, gentlest, rarest, beautiful souls and beings it can turn into its home. True love will find you and will make you its home.

You mustn't lose heart in looking for true love, or you must continue being patient waiting for it. You must never give up the hope that there are still people out there with good hearts and good intentions who can give you the same affection that you give, that there are deserving people you can share the love you have inside with because they will also share all the love they have with you.

You must never give up the hope that you are yet to meet the one who will make you feel so alive, make you experience thrilling moments, and only support you as you thrive. You must hold onto the hope that there is that somebody out there who will make you feel the warmth of the Sun, that there is that someone who will see you and value you for all that you are and all that you aren't, that there is that person who also believes in forever just like you do. They're out there. You need only to believe it's true. They're out there waiting for you. They will find you. You will find them. They will love you. You will love them too.

When you know you are enough,
you will never accept anything in halves,
for you understand it isn't for you
if what they offer doesn't match your
pure, unconditional love.

You must unlearn chasing after love
that isn't meant for you.
you must understand that the best,
the worthy, and the deserving
only arrives when you've learnt to let go.

Sure, love is never late nor is it early,
love arrives exactly when it means to,
but you have to give love a hand
if you are to live the fullest life
you've always dreamed of

and sometimes, to arrive on the other side,
it's not what we keep holding onto,
it's about what we choose to let go
no matter how hard it is for us to do so.

You mustn't be discouraged in looking for or waiting for a great love and you also mustn't despair if ever you don't find it or if you don't stumble upon it out there in our world, for don't you know the truest love you've already found a long, long time ago? All else is but blessings because your truest love is you. You've always had true love already living inside of you, and you'll see this truth if only you would look deep inside of you, and when you do, you'll see, your search for true love has long been through. You've always had your greatest love already buried deep within you. You are your true love, first and foremost. Love your-self so fiercely that you'll be capable of loving others fiercely too.

We're all born alone, we're all alone,
and we'll all die alone.
With this truth, may you learn
to embrace your solitude.
Make a religion out of your melancholy.
Transform your aloneness into an art.
Cherish it, romanticize it, be one with it.
To understand and love yourself
is the path to loving others.

We may not be lonely now and we are not literally alone but we are all, figuratively, incurably, alone. We may have somebody to love and they may be loving us back for the time being, we may have a multitude of family, friends, and admirers but at the end of it all, we're all on our own, and there's no debating that fact.

You see, we came to this world alone and we will leave this place in the same manner. We arrived here with nothing and we will depart unable to carry with us anyone or anything.

Learn to be happy on your own. It is the first step to being happy with another. Learn to be content alone. It is how to be joyful in this world even without the love from another soul.

Learn to be your own savior. It is how to rescue yourself after every hurt or failure. Learn to be one with solitude. It is what will keep you strong. It's what makes everything else more meaningful. It's what makes everything purposeful.

Hold on only to the links, the relationships, the ties that serve your welfare, that strengthen who you are, the people who appreciate your worth, and let go of all the pointless bonds and connections. You will end up in a repetitive rhythm of tears and disappointment if you keep on looking to other people for support and strength.

All the sustenance you need must come from your own self, from exactly your same wavelength and that range can only come from within you. You and only you. There is no one else who can provide you with that depth. You are your only source of power and strength, there is no one else.

Be highly selective of people. You just have to be, especially if you've been through hell multiple times and have it memorized so that you can travel in and out of it without a roadmap and with your eyes closed.

You have to be highly selective of the people you allow to occupy space in your life, most especially if you've been disappointed, let down, and disillusioned far too many times more than a human heart can bear.

Weed out those numbers from a count of many to the fewest who are true to you. You don't need a multitude of lovers, admirers, family, or friends, you only need the ones who genuinely, sincerely, authentically care about you and love you. Quality over quantity. Remember this truth.

You will always be enough for the person who
already learned to love themselves.

If you're chasing after an empty cup,
it's time to wake up and chase after yourself.

You may have been shown what love isn't by the wrong people who played temporary roles in your life story, but when you're finally with the right one, they will show you what real love means, they will show you love's true meaning.

Remember, you are never too much to hold for the right person.

Never lose hope that the most wonderful of humans are out there waiting to hold you as you are, waiting to care for and protect your rare and precious heart.

If the timing is wrong, then the person is wrong.
If the timing is wrong, then 'the love' is wrong.
The timing is not the enemy, the timing is the lesson.

When you're with the right person, you will be happy, things will flow easily, you will never worry, you will never be insecure. With the right person, you will feel comfortable, they will feel like home, you will feel protected, you will feel loved. When you're with the right person, the fear of losing them won't be there to terrify you, for you'll know in your very bones they will never ever leave, that they are there to stay.

When you're with the right one, everything will come as natural as breathing, the love you give may sometimes even be exceeded by the love that you'll receive. When you're with the right one, you will feel complete, you will not question your worth, you will not be confused, you will not ask nor beg for any time or attention. When you're with the right one, you will not wonder about anything, you will finally feel what they mean when they say, "two souls are meant to be."

When you're with the right person, there won't be doubt, only clarity. Yes, there can still be messes but mostly, there is beauty. When you're with the right one, there will be no perplexity, only lucidity.

When you're with the right one, your heart will be nurtured, there will be unconditional love and respect, there will be forgiveness and understanding, there will be vulnerability, admiration, appreciation, trust, and every other good thing that in this world exists.

When you're with the right one, there will be no need to build walls or to create barriers, or put up with anything you don't deserve. When you're with the right one, you will only ever feel yourself continually improve.

When you're with the right one, the two of you together comprise one beautiful whole.

Trust the journey you are on. Trust the ground you're standing upon. You are not advanced, nor behind. You are exactly where you need to be right now. The journey is as important as the destination. The process is the path and the path is the purpose.

You are loved. You may not be aware of it but love is always there for you. You are loved by many; maybe you simply don't pay attention to who they are and how they're there for you. You are loved by the sea and the sky, by the rising and the falling of the waves and the tides. You are loved by the Earth. So what's holding you from demanding the best from yourself? My dearest, you mustn't be afraid to fly. You must never ever be afraid to always try. All the love surrounding you will be the very wind beneath your flight. So fly. Fly.

No matter how alone you are, or how lonely you feel, or how hard things get, remember that you are being safely carried by the arms of Fate, that you only need to open your eyes, you only need to have faith, you only need to believe in all the beauty you are still able to create, you must believe that there are plenty of people around you who can love you whether you have met them or haven't yet, and please know that all the elements surrounding you are radiating the powerful force that is love towards you, believe this to be the truth because love is drawn towards a light that is you.

Love is simply spellbound and drawn towards beautiful humans like you. You are always loved so don't ever give up on loving others too.

May you always appreciate all the love around you. Know that you are loved because you are love itself, you are beauty, you are truth. You are loved because you are enough. You have always been enough. You will always be enough.

In your life, you don't need a large number of lovers, admirers, or friends. In your life, the truth is, you only need one genuine, sincere, authentic connection. You only need one real, solid, secure, enduring, and permanent bond. You only need one stable friendship, one everlasting partnership, only one perpetual relationship. And if you must create a steady, well-built attachment, may you form this first with you. Form this unbreakable bond with yourself firstly before you form it with another soul.

Know thyself, for wisdom lies in this path and no other. Knowing yourself will teach you how to comprehend the world and to unravel the soul of others. It is in knowing yourself that you recognize what is for you and what isn't. It is in knowing yourself that you decipher your purpose, your nature, and your ambition. It is in knowing yourself that you solidify your resilience. It is in knowing yourself that you enable yourself to build a life lived fully. It is knowing yourself that you optimize your human power.

You are the one true fellowship you can always devote all of your love to. You must first establish the strongest, truest bond with your own self. Then the right kind of love will find you. The right kind of love will eventually be attracted to you. The right person will inevitably and inescapably be drawn to you. The right people will stay. The right people will appreciate you. The right people will love you back. But if there isn't anybody, who says that you lack? Who says you're incomplete? Know you're already whole and that it's only yourself you'll ever need.

Only a deserving few will have the courage to attempt to know the depths of you, only a worthy few will attempt to dive into the deepest trenches of your mind and soul, this is why it's okay if you've built a defense to test who wants a serious place within the spaces of your heart, it's okay to filter out so you may let only the worthy ones inside.

May you master the art of discernment and may you find the ones who deserve to experience both the tiniest bits and the colossal pieces of your existence.

You must never apologize for building your heart an impenetrable fortress to protect it from shattering into a thousand pieces. It is understandable that you are only ever protecting yourself from getting hurt, but sometimes, some people are just as terrified as you are, and these are the very people you need to give a chance to, many times if you have to, for they may be the very beings, the very souls made of the same elements as your own soul. You will recognize them because their heart will feel like a home you've known from a long, long time ago.

We've all fallen in love with somebody
whether by choice or by accident,
we've hurt people too,
whether by purposeful intent or unknowingly.
We've all been disappointed
and we've all disappointed somebody.
We've all cried and had caused
someone else's tears to fall,
we've all made mistakes,
we've all committed errors,
we're all only humans and we'll
always make miscalculations,
but at the core of these events
is the lesson that, as humans,
we are capable to receive and to give love,
that love is overall, a decision more than an emotion,
that we can always learn from our errors, and that
we can always be better than who we were before.
This is the power love can do.
This is the wonder love brings to the table.
So allow love to heal you.
Allow love to change you.
Let your self-love save you
so you can then love others too.

We all came from love and love is at the core of our very beings. It is only through society's modernization that we've come up with a culture of loving that teaches us we should not care, that we should 'pretend' not to care, that it's 'cool' not to care, that we should suppress our feelings, that we should not reply immediately to their texts, that we must keep our feelings only to ourselves, that we shouldn't seem too eager, that we should leave immediately the moment that special feeling starts to form inside our bellies, that we should walk away the moment it starts to cause a whirlwind inside our hearts. No, these aren't okay. Why is there a need to hide your heart? Why is there a need to lie about how you feel? When you're not being real, you're betraying who you are.

Modern times taught us that it's okay to jump from connection to connection without first knowing what we want, that it's okay to play mind games with others or to leave unfinished the things that we have begun, that it's okay to leave without explanations, that it's okay to enter connections without first being certain of our own truths, that it's okay to get to know other people without first understanding our own souls, that it's okay to base love on lust, on the surface or the external. But to treat love as a game is not okay, it is never okay, it is disrespectful to yourself and to your fellow humans. Let us not use the word 'love' to define practices that are superficial and let us not define love only to fit our own needs and our selfish wants. Let us not give 'love' the definition that only works for our own benefit. Please only ever create connections that are purposeful and substantial. Please only love when you mean it with all your heart and soul. Do not use love to play relationship games, it is a waste of time. If you want to pursue a connection you think is substantial, by all means, pursue. But do not enter a connection with the mindset of, 'I want to see where this goes' because let me tell you, as a human with a brain for higher reasoning, you can not only see, but you can know. You can be certain which direction all of your love goes.

Let me tell you how it's not okay. It's not okay to pretend you don't love somebody and to play with them these mind games, it's not okay to pretend you don't care when all you want to do is hold them in your arms all night, it's not okay to wait hours to reply to their texts when all you want to do is talk to them all day, it's not okay to treat love as a disposable thing, it's not okay to base love on fantasies, it's not okay to base love on physicality, or trivialities.

Love must have depth, love must be true, you cherish it when love finds you. You embrace it, you try to keep it, you work hard for it, you don't play with it. When the right love comes, you show your person how you truly feel, you don't put on a show, instead, you pour out all the love that you have and know.

You don't take the one you love for granted for pure love is a rare thing. Take good care of it when you've found it for yes, love can be found everywhere but to be blessed with someone who loves you unconditionally is such a precious, unrivaled, incomparable, remarkable thing. Treasure love. Hold onto it. Know true love when it's there because true love is hard to find. True love is rare.

Some things you wanted, you didn't get
for you were meant for something far greater.
Some things you tried to keep, slipped away
for you were being spared of more heartbreak.
Some people you invested in, hurt you
for you were being taught to master
the art of walking away from places
you don't deserve to endure.
For you only deserve goodness,
love, beauty, and truth.

You have to love authentically, you have to love in a way that's sincere. Love is the one thing in this world that would always be worth your time, worth your effort, worth your energy.

Love is what will keep you whole, love is the one thing in this world worth the while, worth the fight, worth to keep, worth holding onto, worth staying for, and worth living for.

So if you must be good at anything in this lifetime, may you master the art of loving.

Never resist love.
Never withhold love.
Love until it aches.
Love until it exhausts you.
To love and be love is what
we've all been sent out here to do.
Let your heart be bruised from loving
and let it mend you too.

They say you must love the way you want to be loved, but before all that, you must first evolve into the person you, yourself, would want to be with. You must first complete the task of accepting yourself, to allow 'who you are' to make peace with 'who you're meant to be.' This is the path to your truth, this is the path to your destiny. This is the road to take to get to where you're supposed to be. Let go of the burdens weighing you, set them all free. Leave your old self behind and your highest self you will meet. When you've evolved into your best self, the right people and the right connections begin to be revealed.

Do not believe Abraham Maslow's claim that sex is a physiological need, no, you do not need sex to survive, it is meant for procreation so our species will not die. Physiological needs are what our physical bodies require to carry out basic functions and to stay alive. You will die without water and food but you will not die without sex. Sex is an impulse, an instinct we are meant to and able to control. Sex entails chemicals that then evoke emotions that lead you to be blinded by a certain situation, person or event. You don't need sex to be happy. There are far more meaningful pursuits and hobbies. Sex is one of the opiums of the masses, a band-aid patch we cover over our existential crises, an excuse from working on the resolutions we must find for ourselves, and issues within us that need to be confronted.

Sex is only meant to be done with the person whom you want to have your children with and raise them with. Sex is done with the person whom you want your children to be like or want them to look up to. Sex is a basic neurological process like eating, sleeping, or drinking, but is not needed for a human body to operate; this impulse can be put under control if one is mentally resilient enough. And as a homo sapien with a neocortex meant to be utilized for higher levels of thinking, you are capable of delayed gratification. Self-discipline, morals, ethics, virtues, and self-care are still the golden keys to the doors that lead to the most fulfillment in this lifetime.

Love is expensive. Sex is cheap. Sex is sometimes free. But love comes at a cost. Love comes at a great price. You must not give your love away just to anyone. Save your love for someone worthy. Save your love for the one who will value it. Love yourself until the right one arrives. Love the one who appreciates you. Love the one who respects you. Love the one who deserves you.

When you have fully embraced who you are as a being, only then will you be ready to give away all the love you have within.

Once you've accepted all your flaws, only then can you be vulnerable to another soul and share with them the madness your soul holds.

Before you fall in love with someone else, please first fall in love with yourself.

First, become the person you want to fall head over heels in love with, the kind of human you'd want to be devoted to.

Allow who you are right now to meet with who you're meant to become. Then you'll see, effortlessly, the right love will come.

'Love' is an undressing of one's soul, a revelation of one's most vulnerable parts, love is an unclothing, an honest disclosing of one's entirety, a confessing, an unraveling, an unfolding, a declaration, an admission, a succumbing. May you always love well, may you always love true. Devote your soul to the one who deserves all of your truth. Devote your heart to the one who also devotes themselves to you.

To show your bare soul to someone is to ask them to love all that you are and all that you aren't, you are asking them to love all the sides and all the angles of your truest self, you are telling them that you are a flawed human being as we all are, and that all these darkest parts need accepting if we are to genuinely and authentically be loved by another soul.

Understanding. This is how love is supposed to be, this is how love is meant to be shown, this is how love is destined to be known. This is what love is created for, this is what love is for. To love is to understand and accept the bare, the raw, the truth, the pure, the light, the dark, the shadows, the beauty, and the nakedness of our souls. Love genuinely. Love wisely. Love like love is all you know. Understand yourself so you can then understand another, for to unravel the deep trenches of someone's being is the first step towards the acceptance of them which then leads to loving their soul as much as you love your own.

When you feel lonely and you feel like the only so-lution is another human being and their attention, please, choose loneliness. True love is never found out of fear of being alone and especially not born out of feeling lonely. Be strong on your own and do the work that needs to be done within you first because when you do, that's when the right love finds you.

Life is too short for you to waste it on the wrong people and things. So between a temporary connec-tion and being alone, choose aloneness, for it is only in solitude that you transform into this all-powerful, resilient human being. It is in the art of being alone that you can grow and flourish.

Why do you want to be anywhere else? Why do you want to be someone else? Why do you want to skip moments of your beautiful life? Know there is beauty even in the struggle. So you must go through the fire, pass through the dark tunnel with all the grace you can muster and with all the courage you can conjure for the only path towards the light is through the shadows.

The universe meant for you to be here, in this exact moment you're living in, it means for you to honor all your chaos and all your glory, it means for you to learn from all the madness and all the beauty. You see, out of the immeasurable potential human beings who could've been in your place, you're here and for this reason, you must relish your existence.

You're supposed to be here, you belong and when the world is making you feel like you don't, you must remember that you are more than what you do for a living, you are more than where you live, you are more than the car you're driving, you are more than your physical body, you are more than how your mind is wired, for you are your soul's beauty, you are more than just a number, you are more than all your fears and anxieties, you are more than what you've left unfinished, you're more than what you've achieved and what you still haven't, you are more than other people's opinions, you are more than how you look, you are more than all your failures and also more than your successes, you are more than anything your mind can bring to life, you are more than anything your potentials can assemble, you are more than all the material things and properties out there you can possess, you are more than any feeling, you are more than any label or judgment or stereotype, you are more than any pain, you are more than the tears, you are more than enough because you are everything.

One day you will wake up in the morning without the nightmares that used to haunt you, one day you will wake up without the darkness that used to scare you, one day you will wake up and the shadows will be right behind you, one day you will wake up and you will feel hopeful of the better days ahead because after all, the best is yet to come, my friend. One day you will wake up in the morning with nothing but happy thoughts inside your head, one day you will wake up and go about your day with the biggest smile on your face, one day you will wake up excited to greet the day, one day you will wake up and find yourself in a beautiful city where they make dreams come alive, one day you will wake up with so much eagerness for life, one day you will wake up to live life so fully not just exist or get by, one day you will wake up and December winters will feel like May, and so my dearest, why not let that day begin today?

Stop flooding other people's hearts with love, instead, flood yours first. Pour all of your love into your own heart until it's overflowing, spilling over, relieving it of all of its thirsts. Outpour all of your emotions, all of your affection to your own heart before to someone else's because you can only give away a love that you've already given to yourself.

Love you first and then you'll see how your love will then flow to the rest of humanity. Isn't this way what Einstein had said is the noblest way to live?

Solitude is sweet. Aloneness is an art. Melancholy is poetic. Loneliness can cure a heart. When you say alone, people taste arsenic, they taste a poison from what truly is an elixir. When you say solitude, people fear, people pity, people judge, people have a distaste for what in reality is the nectar of self-love. Be alone, my dearest, master this gift, be proficient in being solitary, be superior in the art of self-love, for it is in this craftsmanship that you become an expert, a genius, a virtuoso, a real hero of true love and in mastering this skill, you'll then be able to radiate love effortlessly inside and out.

Someone who has the power to be alone yet complete is a force to be reckoned with. They also say someone who is unafraid to dine alone is aware of what they can offer to the table. Someone who shows up strong yet solitary comes off as frightening for they know all the truths of who they are. Someone who loved themselves into wholeness is more powerful than any celestial sky. Be that powerful force by loving yourself first and always, while you're living until the day you die. It's the work that counts, it's what's worthwhile, it's how you can make the most out of your life.

Honor your emotions using your heart but process them using your brain. Let your heart feel but let your mind interpret so you may prevent the two from going to war, for there is a delicate connection, an intricate balance, a fragile link between the heart and the mind. If we aren't careful, the two may destructively collide. Be wise, be perceptive, maintain your soul's equilibrium at all times. Keep a stable ground between reason and emotion, the two are so exquisitely tied.

Emotional intelligence is simply the marriage of the heart and of the mind.

There are times when the world will force you to blend in with the majority, to conform with the popularity, to match up to the world's impossible standards, or to believe and accept truths that your heart does not beat and sing to. Please know you don't need to do these things in order to survive, in order to belong, or in order to be happy. You do not need to change who you are, not for anything or for anybody. You are already beautiful just the way you are. You are enough, you are powerful, you are strong, you are complete so why will you change for anyone else's satisfaction? The only one you need to impress in this world is yourself. The right people will love you and appreciate you for all that you are and all that you aren't. The right people will value all that you're worth.

The only person you need to please about who you are is yourself, there's no need to change parts of your being just because of what other people say or think. Why will you hold yourself from speaking up when you are meant to loudly use your voice? Why are you going to be soft and gentle when you are meant to be wild and fierce? Why are you trying to be invisible when you are meant to stand out and be seen? Why are you underestimating yourself, don't you know you are made of stardust as same as the elements that compose our Sun? Why are you diminishing your light when you are meant to shine so bright?

Do not fear your beauty, do not fear your magnificence, do not fear your potentials, your capabilities, your talents, your gifts—for you are meant to light up the world, and you're meant to share bits and pieces of yourself to inspire others. You are meant to give out the love you've already learned to give yourself. Don't hold back your light from burning. Let it illuminate the darkest places here on Earth.

Be kind to everyone even when they aren't kind to you. We're all fighting a battle we don't proclaim out loud. We're all housing some hurt buried within some quiet little corner of our hearts and some have perfected the art of hiding their pain well. We're all great at covering up our sadness with a smile. We've all uncovered the technique of drawing a veil over our fears and over our tears. We've all learned to camouflage the sorrows that live underneath our skins. So be kind to everyone, but most of all, be kindest to yourself. You can choose kindness each and every day. To be kind is one of the greatest forms of love one can ever learn. Be kind always without expecting kindness in return.

Cherish the honest moments, like the moment when you gasped from a good news you have been waiting for, the moment when you cried tears of joy because you got your prayer, the moment when you looked into someone's eyes and realized you're falling in love, the moment when you had to cry in front of your mother because your best friend had to move away, the moment you first got your heart broken by your childhood crush, the moment you got your heart shattered by your first love, the moment when you got drunk and you kissed an unrequited love, the moment when you woke up one morning and had to take a second to remember you were on a paradise island, the moments when you close your eyes and picture the life of your dreams, the moments when you daydream, that moment when you open up your heart to someone else. Cherish these honest moments for they are fleeting, they quickly come and go. And in every moment, learn the lessons, there's always something you can surely gain and know. Cherish the honest moments. Cherish your life. Cherish it all.

Do not wear a costume, a mask, or a disguise to conceal parts of who you are. Please only ever be true to yourself and only show the world your truth. There is no sense in hiding your beauty, there is no point in diminishing your light, there is no point in holding yourself back, there is no point in shrinking all the skills, the abilities, and all the gifts that you have. There is no sense in being ashamed of all of your flaws for no one is perfect, everyone makes errors. There is no point in hiding the darkest parts of your being for there is no light without the shadows. There is no point in masquerading as someone you are not for you are beautiful the way you are right now. You are enough. Do not wear a camouflage only to blend in and be accepted, for you already belong. You are here, you exist, you're alive, you are needed, you are part of the story, you are loved, you are seen, you are enough, you are worthy, you belong. You belong.

You can be a good friend to others even while you're still working on yourself. Being a good friend doesn't mean you have to always be there for them, that you have to show up day and night, what matters is you're there when they need you the most. It's okay not to be available for them ceaselessly, it's okay because you also have a heart and a soul to protect, you cannot take care of your own being by prioritizing others over yourself. You cannot sacrifice for other people around the clock, you cannot be the one who always compromises, you cannot be the one who endlessly gives away and they're the ones who take every time, this will cause you to burn out faster than a meteorite crashing into the Sun.

It's okay to set boundaries, it's okay to establish limits as to how much weight from other people you are willing to lift, as to how much time you are willing to give, as well as how much of your light you are okay with to emit.

You are not being a bad friend if you only show up for them sometimes, you need moments to be alone and do the greatest work of knowing yourself. It's okay not to be present for your friends all of the time, after all, if they're true, they will have the heart to understand.

Fate would not have allowed you to come this far only for you to give up. So keep moving forward, only ever onwards because you simply can't go back. To lose heart isn't an option for you, it isn't a choice, it isn't a possibility for there is so much more wonder out there for you to see. My dearest, you have in you the power to be the greatest version of who you ever could be and it only takes one choice, one leap. So claim it. Grow into it. Become it. Let it unfold. Set yourself free.

It is easier to notice the things we have lost than the things that have remained. It is much easier for our human nature to see the things that left than the things that stayed. It is much, much easier to focus on the losses than all the wins or all the gains.

These are natural and these are human. But you've been given a higher consciousness to practice gratitude instead of complaining. So please count all the blessings and not the pain. Count the sunshine, not the rain. Don't count what's gone, count what remains. You can be thankful every day, all the time, again and again. Practice gratitude. Always be thankful. There's a rainbow always after the rain.

Maybe someday we'll find what we are looking for, or maybe we won't. Maybe one day we'll end up where we've always hoped for, or maybe we won't. Maybe somehow, somewhere we'll get to our dreams, or maybe we won't. Maybe there's something better than all of the things we've ever imagined for ourselves, better things than anything we could've ever hoped for, better things than anything our hearts could've ever longed for.

Regardless of the ending, the search and the striving should be enough to fill our hearts with the happiness we're all chasing after. All the beauty and meaning are found in the attempt and the struggle, the joy in the eventual attainment is only an extra blessing, one of life's supplementary from what is truly worthwhile. To experience and to live with presence throughout our journey is the main narrative of our lives.

Maybe you are hurting because you are disconnected from something within you. Maybe you have created too far of a distance from who you are now to your innermost truths. Maybe there is a benefit to this hurt and it is to listen to your inner compass, to listen to your inner voice once again. Maybe you are hurting because you have lost who you are. Maybe you are hurting because you need to find yourself again. So look within to find yourself and when you do, you'll most certainly be one with resilience. You will stand up. You will start to walk again. You will head towards healing. Your destination is on the other side of this mountain.

So keep walking.
You can also run, crawl, or fly.
But you must never stop.
You must only keep on going.

Be careful of what you think of yourself for it manifests outwardly. Be careful of the words you say for they become prophecies. The stories that you tell the world and the stories you tell yourself become your truth, become your narrative, become the fortune and the substance your heart keeps.

Only repeat the affirmations, proclaim the promises, and kneel to the prayers you want your soul to reap. Your words and thoughts are prophecies, they are forecasts and predictions of the life you want to live. Your words and ideas are the projections of what your heart is yearning to achieve, they are what your soul longs for, what your entire being is craving to receive.

Only speak loudly of things you want to come true, for words and thoughts are the prophecies we wish into existence that then become the truth.

Who told you you need to be perfect? You only need to be a little better than you were yesterday. Perfect is a myth, perfect doesn't exist. Progress is the word you're looking for. Let your competition be yourself and no one else. Comparison is a dangerous downfall so you mustn't look at other people's gifts, we are all created unique, we all carry our own individual aspects. We are all distinct, all of us an individual, each of us is special, exclusive, and different. No one else exists in this world who is exactly just like you. You are the one and only you. We all must be in awe of each other's rarities for we are all beautiful, we are all extraordinary, we're all contrasting colors, chromatics, tints, tones, shades, and hues. All of us are beautiful, this is one of the universal truths.

"When I'm prettier or skinnier or healthier then I'll be happy. When I get the job, then I'll be happy. When I buy that house, that car, that property, then I'll be happy. When I visit this place, then I'll be happy. When I have this person in my life, then I'll be happy. When I am a better person, a better me, then I'll be happy. When I am famous, I am known, then I'll be happy. When I earn people's acceptance and validation, only then will I be happy. When I have reached all the successes that I want, only then will I be happy."

You see, when you are drowning in the 'then I'll be happy' mindset, you will never be able to appreciate the time that is 'now.' You will constantly be spiraling down the black hole of distressing about the future. You will not be able to abide by the laws of the present moment, but you will be stuck abiding by the laws of useless worry. When you are caught in this mindset, you will not be able to see all the beauty and wonder that is now right in front of you when you are meant to relish this stage your existence is currently passing through. Always choose to embrace beauty. Right now is the perfect time to choose to be happy.

You are meant to enjoy this current season you are in, this present moment you've been given, this stage in your life that you'd have to learn from, this period in your life that you need to pass through. This is the point in your life where you are the version of you you'd need to grow out of, the model of you you'd need to evolve from. So you must imagine yourself like a river of water calmly running, streaming, flowing. Does it worry where it's headed? No— for it already knows it's headed to the great sea, it only embraces its current movement, not the rushing, it's simply coursing freely and steadily. Be a river.

What is for you will find you,
all you need is the courage
to reach back and take its hand.
And when you do,
don't ever let it go.
Don't ever let it go.
You never ever let Destiny go.

Sometimes, just getting out of bed becomes an achievement. Sometimes, arriving on time at work becomes a win. Sometimes, a cup of tea or coffee becomes our soothing friend. Sometimes, a book of poetry helps us to pick ourselves up so we can begin again. Sometimes, to survive another day is something to be so proud of. Sometimes, just answering the phone becomes a great performance. Sometimes, to cry ourselves to sleep and wake up the next morning to then brave the day ahead becomes our greatest feat.

Sometimes, life will swallow you alive and all you can do is just breathe. Life can be tough, life can be brutal, life can be heartless and harsh. But no one can stop you from celebrating your existence, you can always rebel against all the monstrosities of life by showing the world how you're lovely inside and out. Show the world all the wonder, the magnificence, and all the beauty that you are.

Who inspires you to be better, to be kinder, to be more loving? Who brings out the best in you? What are the things that ignite your passions, the things that stimulate your mind, things that burn your very bones, things that start a fire within your soul, that rouse your curiosity, that uplift your spirit? What moves you? Who motivates you to be the best version you could be? Who encourages you to keep pursuing your purpose? Who pushes your growth? What helps you while you change? Who supports your evolution? What keeps you strong in your becoming? What fuels you in your journey? What is your destiny?

Find them.

Find who and what inspires you, excites you, im-proves you and then keep them, live for them, love them, fight for them. Inspire them too.

Take yourself to date nights. Take yourself out shop-
ping. Take yourself to watch a movie, take yourself
on trips, by yourself, go see the world. Take yourself
to eat fast food and then to the nicest restaurant you
know; take yourself to libraries, take yourself to mu-
seums, take yourself to coffee shops, take yourself
out to aquariums and nature itself. Be your own best
friend, be your own confidant, be your own therapist,
be your own lover, be your own hero until the end.
If you are to romanticize anything in this life, please
romanticize loving yourself. Inspire yourself, arouse
yourself. Work your dreams into existence, believe in
all the power and all the hope that your heart holds,
protect your mind and your soul, love your halves
and love your wholes, accept your narrows and your
wides, love your desires, love your goals. Embrace your

solitude, embrace being alone, turn your melancholy into poetry, turn your loneliness into a religion, never be ashamed for being a singular noun, it is something to be so proud of. Climb the tallest buildings, conquer the highest mountains, reach for the skies; the limit isn't what we see, the limit is a lie, the limit doesn't exist, so strive for all the aspirations your heart is asking for you to reach. You are amazing; you are beautiful; you are enough. Love yourself whether you're broken or rebuilt, perfect or faulty, immaculate or blemished, up or down, low or high. Love yourself truly, sincerely, love yourself until the day you die. Love your nature, live your purpose; you are all you have. Love yourself so great that you give away effortlessly all the love you have inside. Romanticize loving yourself, my dearest; it is the endeavor most worthwhile.

It is a certainty that you will have to outgrow certain people, places, and things. This happens to everyone who undergoes the process of changing, of transforming, of becoming. As you transition, you will learn you'll have to let go of the people who don't see the same things that you see, people who don't appreciate you are both the sky and the sea, people who don't love you back so fiercely the way that you love them truly. As you grow, you will learn you'll have to let go of all the painful memories and to keep only the lessons. As you move on, you will learn that you'll have to release from your grasp all the places and things that hold you back from your breakthroughs, to let go of the situations that hinder your metamorphosis, and to let go of the attachments that weigh you down from your flight. As you grow, you will most definitely outgrow certain people, places, and things all for the simple reason that they refuse to learn, to progress, and to embrace their own becoming. You don't need anyone's permission to move forward, you can leave behind those who want to stay behind. Know that the decision to advance without some people is the painful price of growing up.

Why do you feel alone? You don't have to feel this way. Don't you see, you are surrounded by love in all forms? Don't you see Earth's Sun shining bright above you, with all certainty to rise and set for you each day? Don't you see Earth's Moon in all its beauty and its glory, changing phases to impress you every night? Don't you see the tiny orbs of light in the vastness of the night sky, reminding you how you're composed of stardust too? Don't you see our planetary seasons leap from winter to spring to summer to fall, a reminder of the impermanence of all things in life, that the only constant in our reality is change? Don't you see that the storms cleanse your vision, that earthquakes shake you when you're comfortable, and that wildfires renew your soul? Do you see, my dearest, you are loved by the entire Universe? Do you feel it carrying you safely in its arms? Remember, all the love you need you already own, that within your heart are worlds and galaxies so there's no need to feel alone.

When your whole world is crumbling into pieces and you are on the verge of giving up, don't. When you feel like retreating to hide underneath the shadows, don't. For you must remember, it is exactly in these moments that you have to be brave because this will be you stepping into the light from out of the cave. You need not ask anybody else for courage, you've always had it in you all along. When you're scared, sing to yourself the lullaby our mothers used to sing us all to sleep when we were young, "Be brave, little one."

Have courage. Be strong. Take Heart. Hold on.

There will be days when you'll feel confused and that's okay. There will be days when you'll doubt yourself and that's also okay. Naturally, you will ask questions and search for the answers but please be patient with your transformation, for at the end of this process, you will be able to strengthen your self-awareness and you will further understand yourself.

Your patience with your heart will be rewarded greatly. Sometimes, you need only to give yourself some grace.

Sometimes, you need only to trust the process.

On days when you don't trust your capabilities or when someone is making you feel inadequate, you must remember you already have everything you need inside yourself and that will always be enough. You must remember to never seek validation from external sources because, at the end of the day, all they offer is a superficial and temporary euphoria.

The only validation that will be long-lasting is the one that comes from within. Always remember you are more than enough, for you are everything.

On days you are being fed the lie that you are difficult to love, difficult to deal with, difficult period, you must remember the truth that you are love itself, that you are love embodied. Sometimes, you'll be the one finding it difficult to love others, and when you're faced with days like these, remember that you don't need to learn compassion, you were already born with it as well as sympathy and kindness burrowed in all of your parts, you need only to use them, you need only to use your heart.

Your worth is not dictated by those who don't have the capacity within them to love you. Sometimes, the very people we expect to catch us when we fall are the very people who pushed us off the cliff. Sometimes, we give away our hearts to those who do not appreciate the immensity of the love that it can give.

Sometimes, we expend so much of our efforts towards somebody who only gives us back half-measures, draining us of all the light we have within. Sometimes, you are the giver and they are the taker.

Know they aren't mistakes, they are the lessons and the catalysts that you exactly needed and were sent for you to learn. And at present, if you are emptying your heart for another, maybe it is time to return your own heart to your ribcage, to where it rightfully belongs, maybe it's time to spend all your energy back towards your entire being, time to emit back to yourself all the light you have been giving someone else.

Maybe it's time to give back to yourself all the love you contain within. If your heart isn't inside your chest, it's clear it's time to love yourself again.

Do not keep running from yourself by constantly attaching yourself to temporary people. You must confront the truth of who you are, you must first understand and meet yourself before you can genuinely build a relationship that's substantial. Before you wholeheartedly embark on one of life's greatest gifts and adventures, which is the opportunity to give and receive love from another heart, make sure you are whole yourself, make sure you are healed, make sure you are prepared, make sure you are resilient, make sure they are the right one, make sure you're the right one.

The character, the mind, the heart, the soul of some-one compose their entirety as a person and the beauty of all the aforementioned lies in how delicate but strong they are, for there should be softness in the heart, resilience in the mind, virtues in the character, and purpose in the soul. May you find the one who possesses all these or may they find you. And please promise yourself, you'll never settle for a soul or for anything less than what your heart deserves.

Believe the truth that it is better to be alone than be with the wrong one because the right one will love you back, the right one will stand out and will be recogniz-able, the right one will be a breath of fresh air, the right one will feel like home, the right one won't make you question, the right one is not confusing, the right one is consistent, the right one is true, the right one wants you, the right one will inspire you, the right one will transform you, the right one will challenge you in ways that will help you to become the best version of you, the right one will grow together with you and not hold you back, the right one will be there for you, the right one will walk side by side with you down the right track.

Please do not fall for the temporary, but reserve your heart only for your evermore. Never fall for superfici-ality, but please fall in love with depth. Please fall for the soul and not for anything else.

It's a winding road that leads to worthwhile destinations, and in this life, no one promised us a straight, safe, or pleasant path. Certainly, there will be twists and turns, perilous rivers, and perhaps many treacherous mountain passes. The beautiful truth is that no one may stop us from enjoying the views of the highlands and of the valleys, of the lakes and of the waterfalls. Our life trajectory is all ours to create, we have the power to choose which of the diverged roads we'd want to tread. I hope you choose the path that is not only what you desire, but what will also make all the difference in your life.

On days you feel most misunderstood, you must remember that people only perceive from the level of their comprehension and from what their heart is willing to receive. You cannot explain to a snake what legs are for because all it knows is how to slither, you cannot make a fish understand flying for it's made of scales and not of feathers. Please remember you hold in you the power to be the one who always understands. Your mind is limitless, your mind is broad, it's wide open, it's understanding, your mind is the one in full command.

On days you feel discouraged and no one seems to believe in all the dreams that you hold, please remember that within you are a billion rising suns that shine like gold. When people don't see what you see, be reminded that in order to chase your dreams, you need not convince anybody, you need not ask permission from anyone else, you must only keep on, you must only be strong, you must only continue forward.

Most people only see what 'is' but you, you have the vision of the 'will be' and it is for this very reason that you must keep on carrying on for that dream is waiting for you, that dream is longing for you, that dream is waiting to come true.

That dream that you see beyond today will be the very thing that gets you through.

Let your dreams save you.

One must go through a death of some sort in order to be resurrected into a new life. Of course, it will be painful. When has dying ever been easy and to be reborn a walk in the park?

Turn the page and live your next chapter with all the love and courage your heart can muster.

Turn the page and stop rereading the last chapter, your best adventure has only begun.

Please promise yourself to be unafraid to live again.

There is no need to worry about the things that have not yet passed. It is useless panicking about the events that may or may not be. Worrying has never changed the course of the future, doing one's best to achieve one's desired outcome definitely has. But if you must overthink over something, overthink on all the goodness and all the things within your grasp.

Why lose sleep over the inevitable? There is no point wasting your energy on things you cannot control. What if everything turns out to be more beautiful than what you have imagined, than what you have asked for, longed for, yearned for, or ever hoped for? Maybe you must be worried about being over-whelmed by all the wonderful possibilities. Please don't lose sleep over anything, but if you must, lose sleep only over your dreams, lose sleep only over all the beautiful, wonderful things.

There is beauty in being lost and in the desire to simply pause. It is perfectly okay to be afraid of all the uncertainty, it is okay to admit that you want to rest your exhausted heart, it is okay to just breathe. It's okay to rest a bit, to put down all the weight you're carrying for even just a little while, to take a break from the journey and simply enjoy the wonders surrounding you as you search for what's worthwhile.

It's okay to say no to the things that don't provide fuel to your forward motion. It's okay to leave behind unnecessary baggage if they are only slowing the progress you're trying to make. It is acceptable for you to ignore all the distractions trying to halt your further advancement in the journey you've decided to take.

The best of the best moments in your story may still lie a little bit further down the road, this is why you cannot ever turn back and you cannot ever give up, for it is not about the distance nor the speed, it is all about stepping one foot forward each time you have the strength to do so as you breathe. Lightly, you can take things gently if you need to, there is nothing wrong with that. Even angels fall, even heroes bleed, even the greatest warriors have lost battles.

Tread the road at your own pace. Life isn't a race. Take it one step at a time. Take it one day at a time. Progress is a victory no matter how small. Each little step you take is already a triumph.

Your words or actions may just be exactly what they needed to hear or see or read for them to take the leap and change where they currently are, eventually leading them to change their lives. This is why if you know in your very heart and feel in your very bones the reason you were born here on Earth for, chase after it, live it, be it, please never stop and never give up. You must keep going because you don't know just who you are inspiring and you don't know just who you are leading out of the darkness and towards the light.

Live your purpose.
Live your nature.
Be who you are.

We humans are messy creatures—we lust, we crave, we sin, we hurt, we suffer, we harm each other, we yearn, we hunger, we desire, we thirst, we want, we pine, we itch, we covet, but we can also love.

Love is our one rescue from all the sins listed above. Love is the one thing that can save you, love is the one and only good thing in our lives. Give love. Be love. Live in love. Learn from love. Be better because of love.

All the love you'll ever want and need you already have.

True beauty doesn't need attention, external valida-
tion, assurance, affirmation, confirmation, or outside
acceptance because something truly beautiful is sim-
ply, quietly, and undeniably, present.

True beauty is not loud, it's not arrogant nor proud,
it doesn't boast. It is tranquil, it is still. True beauty
is silently existing but with a presence that echoes
magnificence and inspiration.

True beauty is kindness, true beauty is in forgiveness,
true beauty is in generosity, true beauty is in loyalty,
integrity, and modesty, true beauty is peace, true beau-
ty is calmness, true beauty is composure and grace,
true beauty is found in the virtuous embellishments of
one's heart, true beauty resides in all the wisdom con-
quering one's mind, true beauty is in the loveliness of
one's soul, true beauty is in the character, true beauty
is in one's strength, true beauty rests in one's wounds
that you have chosen to heal.

True beauty is in persistence, true beauty is resilience,
true beauty lies in being yourself, true beauty is living
your truth, true beauty is knowing your worth, true
beauty is living your nature, true beauty is fulfilling
your purpose, true beauty is already buried deep in-
side of you. True beauty, my dearest, is you.

It takes courage to stand up for everything your heart believes in, for what your soul is passionate about, for what you want to live for. It takes bravery to go against the current, to chart your own course, to think for yourself, to be your true self, and to embrace that self. It takes so much determination to chase after your dreams. It takes selflessness to share what you have and be generous to others. It takes boldness to accept your uniqueness. It takes so much power to be strong in a world that constantly pressures to change who you are by trying to blend you in right into its mediocrity. It takes a resilient heart and mind to shine like the Sun. So be mentally and emotionally intelligent, my dearest, for this is how the wars inside us and outside us are won.

Whenever you fall,
you can always rise.
You must promise yourself
to be better each time.

You must care for your own heart, you must look after your own soul, you must protect your mind because the most important, indispensable, essential person you have in this world and in your life is you. You and only you.

There is no other force in this Universe you can channel towards yourself that is more powerful, more healing, more transformative, or more profound than the love already living inside your own heart.

You are more than enough. You are worthy. Radiate out from your heart all the love you carry.

May you never look for love in the wrong places, for it can only be found within yourself. May you never trade in your self-respect for love and affection from another person's heart. May your mindset always be "I have the power to walk away from anything that does not serve my highest good." May your heart be so resilient it can always stand alone. May you only form relationships that are real, that are healthy, that are strong, that grow you, support you, and love you too. May you only surround yourself with things, situations, and people who deserve all of your precious energy and love. May you always be sure of what you're worth. May you always put yourself first before anything or anyone else in this world, for during the times you're in need of redemption or salvation, only you can save yourself.

CHARIS ED is, by profession, an Oncology RN and, by nature, a writer and poet. When not administering chemotherapy, Charis can be found either chasing dreams or seeking solace in between the pages of a book. She believes in the transformative power of words.

instagram.com/charised_